KU-528-203

The New Politics
of
Criminal Justice

ANN JAMES AND JOHN RAINE

LONGMAN
LONDON AND NEW YORK

Addison Wesley Longman Limited
Edinburgh Gate
Harlow, Essex CM20 2JE
England

and Associated Companies throughout the world

*Published in the United States of America
by Addison Wesley Longman Inc., New York*

© Addison Wesley Longman Limited 1998

The right of Ann James and John Raine to be identified
as the authors of this work has been asserted by them in accordance
with the Copyright, Designs and Patents Act 1988.

All rights reserved; no part of this publication
may be reproduced, stored in a retrieval system, or transmitted in
any form or by any means, electronic, mechanical, photocopying,
recording, or otherwise without either the prior written permission of
the Publishers or a licence permitting restricted copying in the United
Kingdom issued by the Copyright Licensing Agency Ltd,
90 Tottenham Court Road, London W1P 9HE

First published 1998

ISBN 0 582 31721-5 Paper

British Library Cataloguing-in-Publication Data

A catalogue record for this book is
available from the British Library

Set by 7 in 10/12 sabon
Printed and bound by CPI Antony Rowe, Eastbourne
Transferred to digital print on demand, 2006

Dedication

*This book is dedicated to the late Michael Willson,
our mutual friend and inspiration. Days before he died
from cancer, at the age of just 47, Michael expressed his
desire that we should write a volume together on criminal
justice, a subject about which he cared passionately.
It is with Michael's sense of justice and equity that we
have approached this volume.*

Ann James and John Raine
Spring 1998

Authors' Acknowledgements

We acknowledge, with gratitude, the support of all the staff at Addison Wesley Longman in this project.

Publisher's Acknowledgements

We are indebted to the following for permission to reproduce copyright material:

The controller of Her Majesty's Stationery Office for permission to reproduce Table 1.1 'The impact of the criminal justice process' from *Trends in Crime, Findings for the 1992 British Crime Survey, Research findings No. 14* by Mayhew, Mirrlees-Black and Maung (1994), Crown Copyright

Contents

CONTENTS

PART I

CHAPTER ONE

Crime and criminal justice

1.1 Introduction

This is a book about the policy and practice of criminal justice. It is therefore not so much a book about crime as about responses to crime; responses by the state, by its agencies and by its citizens to crime and to the perceived threat to social order which crime represents. The volume addresses three main questions: What is the contemporary purpose of criminal justice? What influences have shaped criminal justice in recent years? What does this discussion tell us about criminal justice for the future?

In asking these questions the volume is very much a product of its time and place. It confines its evidence and its search for meaning to the UK (and to England and Wales in particular) during the last quarter of the twentieth century. It does so because of the curious character of criminal justice in the UK at that time, compared with what had gone before.

At first sight the picture of criminal justice during the period presents as unclear and inconsistent. It is marked by disjuncture in direction and rapid legislative and policy change. Between 1979 and 1997, for example, Parliament debated at least one major piece of legislation originating from the Home Office every session, compared with just five Acts of equivalent significance in the previous fifty years (Wasik and Taylor, 1994).

Certainly law and order had always been high on the public policy agenda, as reflected in the high status long accorded to the Home Secretary within the Cabinet. But generally this relied upon a measure of consensus between parties in government and in opposition about what was to be done about crime and criminal justice and who was to do it.

There lies the curiosity. In the last two decades of this century issues of law and order increasingly captured public attention and, in turn, became one of the most compelling social issues for politicians. And yet, apart from the political rhetoric, responses to those issues focused on the *workings* of criminal justice rather than on its *purpose*. The primary concern of the period was how to make criminal justice more effective in tackling crime. Solutions were mainly directed at enhancing the efficiency of individual agencies and requiring them to work together as a single 'criminal justice system'. The 'how?' questions inevitably took precedence over the 'what?' or 'why?' questions.

The distinctive contribution of this volume is to begin to reconnect the functioning of criminal justice with its purpose and direction. In doing so, the volume raises difficult and even uncomfortable questions about how and why criminal justice policy was constructed in such a form over the period, about where criminal justice happens, about the role of the public as active participants in the process, and about possible ways forward, not least under a new Labour government. In making its case, the volume deconstructs both traditional and post-modernist theory and analyses the contributions of some key contemporary thinkers in criminal justice.

The primary thesis of the book is that criminal justice policy and practice in the period under review has been shaped by the presence and interplay of four key dynamics (Figure 1.1). These are identified as politicisation (Chapter 2), managerialism (Chapter 3), administrative processing (Chapter 4) and public voice and participation (Chapter 5). It is argued that each dynamic has contributed its own logic and rationale based on its own set of values, each has made its own distinctive mark on policy and practice, and each has its own legitimacy, though each is often at odds with the others. Of particular interest and significance are the dynamics of administrative processing and public voice and participation, the influence of both of which, it is proposed, have been underestimated in other contemporary analyses of criminal justice, compared with the more overt pressures of politicisation and managerialism during and since the Thatcher reforms. The tensions and conflicts between these four dynamics, it is argued, begin to explain the curious nature, the inconsistencies and the disjunctures within criminal justice at the time.

In presenting this thesis, the book begins by identifying the na-

4

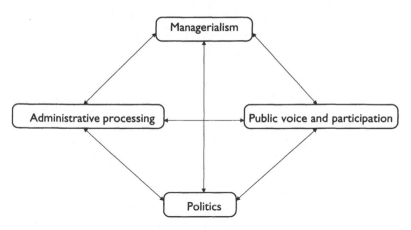

Figure 1.1 The dynamics shaping criminal justice

ture of the problem to be addressed – namely, the problem of crime and the incapacity of criminal justice policy and practice to resolve it. It proceeds to identify the primary and competing paradigms which have traditionally both bounded and shaped the nature of discourse within criminal justice and the forms in which those paradigms have been revisited and reworked during the period under review.

Part I of the volume focuses on the period 1979–1997 (the eighteen-year period of Conservative government in the UK). Part II looks to the millennium and beyond. In doing so, it builds from an untidy mix of policies and structures and picks a careful way through contemporary literature and a post-market paradigm to identify a rationale and key features of a possible way forward. That way forward is presented tentatively not as a solution but as a contribution to the debate on and about criminal justice. Whether or not the suggested way forward meets the expressed criteria of Labour's Home Secretary – of a criminal justice system that is 'fair, swift and effective' (Straw, 1997) – remains to be seen.

1.2 The problem of crime

Criminal justice in the period under review was facing a mounting crisis because of its perceived failure to resolve, or indeed reduce, the problem of crime (Uglow, 1995; Muncie and McLaughlin,

LIVERPOOL JOHN MOORES UNIVERSITY
LEARNING SERVICES

1996). The enhanced profile given to the problem of escalating crime rates by politicians, by the public and by the media in the 1980s and early 1990s confronted all concerned with the perceived failure in a particularly dramatic way. While politicians looked for radical and simple solutions, practitioners became overwhelmed by the conflicting demands of overwork and perceived under-performance. That public concerns about crime were rising, even in years when official statistics were reporting a fall in the volume of recorded crime, presented a significant problem for politicians (McLaughlin and Muncie, 1996; Downes, 1997).

Violent crime was a particular concern, but public perceptions of a society increasingly drifting towards lawlessness were also amplified by worries about the threat of serious public disorder, frequency of incidence of domestic burglary, of children beyond control, of drug cultures and of 'no go' areas, of terrorism, of hooliganism, and of vandalism. It was a view widely shared not only by those who had been victims of crime, but also by those fortunate to have avoided, so far, its direct effects and by many of those who made their living as professionals within the criminal justice agencies. Accompanying this perception was an increasing fear of being victimised, such that fear of crime came to be ranked among the top subjects of anxiety in most public opinion polls conducted in the 1990s (MORI, 1996).

Official statistics tended to justify this pessimistic outlook. From the 1930s onwards, the number of crimes recorded by the police increased almost every year. But from the mid-1950s, the rate of increase escalated markedly (Figure 1.2). The greatest increase in the rate occurred in the 1980s and early 1990s – from 2.4 million recorded offences in 1979 to 5.4 million in 1992.

Almost certainly these figures underestimated significantly the real extent of crime in society. For many years the reliability of of-ficial crime statistics as a measure of criminality had been ques-tioned on the grounds that they ignored unreported crime and crimes reported but unrecorded by the police. For this reason the Home Office began in 1982 to conduct separate surveys of crime (the British Crime Survey) through random sampling of the popu-lation. Six such surveys had been undertaken by 1997 and each found official police statistics to have underestimated crime by a factor of almost four. The 1996 British Crime Survey, for example, estimated a total of 19.1 million crimes in 1995. Both official police statistics and the British Crime Survey revealed that most

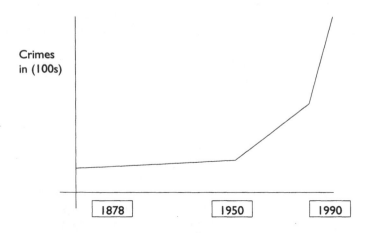

Figure 1.2 Trends in crime in England and Wales

crimes were committed against property (burglary, thefts, vandalism to vehicles and homes accounting for about three out of every four crimes committed), and that crimes against the person accounted for less than a quarter (common assaults formed 15 per cent of all crime in 1995, and theft from the person accounted for less than 4 per cent, while violent crime comprised slightly over 6 per cent (Home Office, 1996b)).

Both the police statistics and the British Crime Surveys showed crime rates to be much higher in lower income, urban, communities. In such areas, more people were likely to be repeatedly victimised – a vulnerability often compounded by the victims' poverty and inability to take preventative steps and by the failure of official agencies to provide adequate protection or to deal effectively with the perpetrators of crime. The surveys highlighted how such areas were often characterised by high levels of anti-social behaviour and public nuisance, augmenting fear and expectation of being victimised. But the statistics showed that crime was not only a phenomenon of poor and urban areas. Middle-class neighbourhoods in cities would also be obvious targets for property crime and all the surveys showed crime to be of no less concern among communities in rural areas. Indeed, fear of crime in such areas was found to be heightened by isolation and, ironically, by the relative

7

infrequency of its incidence, just as exposure to repeated crime and risk tended to deaden anxiety and sense of vulnerability. And although urban areas experienced far higher levels of crime against property, reflecting the greater opportunities for theft and burglary, violent crime had the potential to affect anyone anywhere. Domestic violence, the most under-reported form of crime (Mirrlees-Black, 1994), respected neither class nor geography, though its victims would be predominantly female. Bullying in schools, research indicated, similarly was commonplace in middle-class and working-class environments (Department of Education and Employment, 1995).

The analyses conclude that crime is a predominantly male phenomenon (some 83 per cent of known offenders were male in 1989). It is also shown to be a phenomenon concentrated upon the relatively young. One-third of all men born in the early 1950s had a criminal conviction by the age of 31, and the peak age for offending in 1992 was 18 for males and 15 for females. The majority of crime is therefore concentrated upon a relatively small proportion of the population. About 3 per cent of offenders were estimated to be responsible for more than a quarter of all offences (Graham and Bowling, 1995). Although some 55 per cent of young men and 31 per cent of young women admitted to committing a crime at some time during their lives, most committed only one or two offences.

The analyses also showed that young people are most likely to be victims of personal crime, older teenagers bearing the highest risk of assault. Three-quarters of young people convicted of the most violent and serious offences and held in secure care or custody had themselves been victims of physical, sexual or emotional abuse (Boswell, 1995).

1.3 Criminal justice agencies

The contemporary tasks of criminal justice agencies can be described as, first, to protect the public; second, to administer justice; third, to manage penalties imposed on those found guilty of breaking the law; and, fourth, to manage the process of reintegration into the community and the promotion of law-abiding behaviour after punishment. Within this overall framework of purposes, the major proportion of activity, and therefore of public spending devoted to criminal justice, has long been directed towards the apprehension and prosecution of those suspected of committing crimes.

The task of *protecting the public* has traditionally been identified primarily with the police, who are expected to be active in preventing crime (for example, by street patrols) as well as to respond swiftly and effectively when offences are committed. Protecting the public is also, however, one of the key functions of the prison service, which undertakes a key role in relation to the task of managing penalties imposed on offenders. More recently, the task of protecting the public has been directly associated with local authorities as agents of community safety (Bright, 1997). It has also been recently identified as a primary function of the Probation Service (Straw, 1997) in relation to assessment of risk which particular offenders represent to the public, in providing security for the public in the administration of community penalties, and in informing victims of prisoners' release.

The task of *administering justice* lies at the core of the criminal justice process, with the focus traditionally upon the courts. Here the prosecution and defence present their evidence and information to the court which adjudicates on guilt or innocence and determines the sentence for those found guilty. In England and Wales, about 97 per cent of all criminal cases are dealt with in the magistrates' courts before a lay bench, typically comprising three justices of the peace who decide both guilt or innocence and sentence. More serious cases (indictable offences, and some of those classified as triable 'either way') are transferred to the Crown Court where they are heard by a judge and jury (the judge directing the process and determining the sentences of those convicted; the jury determining guilt or innocence). In addition to the courts, however, the police and other authorities have taken on an increasingly significant role in administering justice through the exercise of powers to 'caution' suspected offenders instead of pursuing a prosecution through the courts and through the use of 'administrative penalties' (for example, fixed penalties for various motoring offences).

The task of *managing penalties* in custody and in the community is usually associated with the prison and probation services, although in practice the most common form of penalty is a monetary fine, collected directly by the courts. Whereas traditionally the management of penalties has been a function wholly undertaken by state agencies, increasingly, the task has involved the independent sector, both in the operation of privately-run prisons and of probation programmes run in partnership with the voluntary sector.

Finally, the task of *managing the process of reintegration into the community and the promotion of law-abiding behaviour after punishment* has traditionally fallen to the probation service although, increasingly, this is becoming a role for other agencies as well, including the courts, as interest in 'restorative justice' and in 'reparation' has grown (NACRO, 1997).

The period under review is marked by the apparent incapacity of criminal justice agencies to be seen to deliver successfully on these four core functions. For example, the British Crime Survey, 1994, reported that only 5 per cent of crimes estimated to be committed against individuals and their property were cleared up and only 3 per cent resulted in a formal outcome – a caution by the police or a conviction by the courts (Table 1.1).

If the problem of crime was increasing, particularly during the 1980s and early 1990s, the capacity of criminal justice agencies to address it was not keeping pace. That criminal justice agencies should be regarded as responsible for resolving the crime problem was in itself, of course, unrealistic, and arguably a function of over-promising by politicians and agencies which had begun much earlier (Chapter 2). Criminal justice agencies had, it seems on reflection, colluded with the politicians and public who had invested them with the responsibility, authority and potency to address crime. But if the problem for politicians and the public was that of crime, the problem for criminal justice agencies was of purpose and identity. If the criminal justice process and criminal justice agencies could not reduce crime, what were their nature and pur-

Table 1.1 The impact of the criminal justice process

Offences committed	100%
Offences reported	47%
Offences recorded	27%
Offences cleared up	5%
Offences resulting in a caution or conviction	3%
Offences resulting in a conviction	2%

(Mayhew, Mirrlees-Black and Aye Maung, 1994)

pose? There followed a series of initiatives designed to enhance the efficiency of criminal justice agencies in addressing crime; initiatives broadly consistent with the managerialist thrust of the Thatcher years (Chapter 3). The result was that, while criminal justice began to look more like a system for the management of crime, it became increasingly uncertain about its purpose. It was this situation of uncertainty which reinforced and made explicit a polarisation of views around the two traditional contrasting paradigms for criminal justice: those of 'welfare' and 'justice'.

1.4 Contrasting paradigms in criminal justice

The 'welfare' paradigm begins from the position of the offender and asks the question: 'Why did this offender commit this crime?' Depending upon the answer (and there are many), a solution is constructed to prevent further offending on the part of the individual or others perceived to be in similar circumstances. The result is a perspective, or a series of perspectives, that focus on three aspects: resolution of the causes of crime, adjustment in the behaviour of those who offend, and the rehabilitation into the community of offenders. The 'justice' paradigm, in contrast, begins from the position of the crime committed and sometimes additionally from the person offended against – namely, the citizen or victim or, through their representative, the law enforcer. It asks the question: 'What is the appropriate penalty for this offence?' Again, a solution is constructed, but here according to perceptions of what is just ('justice') and fair and what is likely to deter the offender (or offenders in similar circumstances) from reoffending. The result is one, or a series of perspectives which are retributionalist and which may or may not additionally include a restorative function.

The welfare perspective emerged in the early 1960s, contemporary with the influence of psychology, sociology and politics in social policy, and subsequently dominated criminology and much of criminal justice practice until the 1980s in the UK. There were three strands to the perspective. Psychology concentrated on the individual, on individual behaviour and on resolving criminal behaviour at the individual level. Sociology and social psychology, known collectively as 'deviancy theory', concentrated on the individual in relation to their environment, and looked for resolution through amending the relationship between the two. Politics concentrated on the structural conditions and ideologies which were perceived as giving rise to crime, and for change in these conditions and ideologies. Together the three strands were mutually reinforcing and provided a powerful rationale for attending to the causes of crime (see Figure 1.3).

The essence of the 'justice' perspective, lately reincarnated within the UK, was captured most famously in Michael Howard's provocative sound-bite to the Conservative Party Conference in Autumn 1993 that 'prison works!'. This challenged the dominant welfarist viewpoint that had prevailed at the Home Office in the preceding years and, indeed, the conventional wisdom among many criminal justice practitioner groups, the police generally excepted. It also challenged the sound-bite of a previous Conservative Home Secretary, Douglas Hurd, who had asserted that 'prison only makes bad people worse'. The effectiveness of custody thus became a hologram of much wider issues about how to respond to the problem of crime in society.

The 'get tough' approach which Michael Howard advocated in 1993 may have represented a considerable challenge to large parts of the practitioner community in the UK and to policy-makers within his own department. But the approach was already well established in the USA, and many of the initiatives which Michael Howard commissioned were drawn directly from experience across the Atlantic. Somewhat ironically, it was a self-proclaimed libertarian – Charles Murray, an American academic – who expressed most persuasively the argument that the UK should follow the lead given in some parts of the United States (Murray, 1990, 1994). His commentaries on the rising crime problem in the UK and his thesis that the welfare model which had dominated criminal justice policy over the preceding thirty years or so had much to do with this, provided much fuel for politicians, of the left as well as the right, who were keen to claim the title of the party of 'Law and Order' (Newburn, 1995).

The underlying thesis of Murray was, in many respects, little more than a reworking of the ideas propounded several years earlier by John Dilulio and his teacher, James Q. Wilson, whose book *Thinking about Crime* had been widely read and influential within American criminal justice circles (Wilson, 1975).

But in terms of the relation of the ideas to the UK context, Murray's contribution to the debate has undoubtedly been important. This contribution has been heightened by its timeliness: it came to-

Psychological

Model	Biological and genetic	Psychodynamic	Behavioural and learning	Learning and cognitive
Theory	Behaviour is determined biologically and genetically	Behaviour may have unconscious origins and always has meaning	Behaviour is stimulus-responsive and can be relearned	Patterns of thinking influence behaviour. Patterns of thinking can be relearned
Key exponents	Conrad Lorenz, Eysenck	Freud	Skinner, Pavlov, Harlow	Piaget
Examples of use in criminal justice	'Unfit to plead' 'Life' sentences	Some psychiatry and counselling	Behaviour modification programmes, Parole	Cognitive therapy programmes

Sociological and political

Model	Labelling	Control	Strain	Conflict
Theory	People will respond to the label placed on them by others	We would all break the law without control measures to stop us	Law-breaking is a rational response by some to unequal access to shared economic and social goals	Lawbreaking is a response to oppression by some over others
Key exponents	Cohen and Young		Durkheim	Marx
Examples of use in criminal justice	Decriminalisation and 'down-tariffing' of offences	Surveillance, tracking, home and car security and other deterrence measures	Linking of crime with unemployment, poverty and poor housing	Equal opportunities. Crowd control

Figure 1.3 Traditional welfare models in criminal justice practice

wards the end of an uninterrupted eighteen-year period of Conservative government in the UK. The essence of Murray's argument is of a connection between the rate of use of custody as a sentence and the level of crime, this being apparent to Murray in the statistical trends in both the UK and the USA (Murray, 1997).

Murray has highlighted the marked decline in the use of custody in the USA that took place in the 1960s and an apparently corresponding increase in the rate of crime, followed by a shift in policy in the early 1970s under which the USA increasingly sent criminals to prison. Whereas in 1974 the number of prisoners in state and federal prisons was just over 218,000, by 1979 it was over 300,000, by 1983 it was 400,000 and by 1986, 500,000. Since that year, the USA has been imprisoning about 50,000 people every year, and in 1995 the prison population was in excess of 1 million.

Murray's own analysis has *not* shown this trend to have been accompanied by a corresponding reduction in crime, and he has acknowledged that the relationship is more complex. His argument, however, has been that imprisonment is vital to crime control, and here the statistical analysis of more recent trends in the UK has lent some reinforcement because decline in use of custody through the 1960s, 1970s and 1980s coincided with a steady and equivalently significant rise in the crime rate.

Two particular lessons which Murray has drawn from the American experience, and which he has presented as applicable to the UK, are as follows. First, he argues that reducing the use of custody does affect crime rates insofar as, in the early 1960s in the USA, the use of custodial sentencing was falling *ahead* of increases in crime. Murray has also argued that an analysis of the American experience in the 1970s and 1980s misses the point that it has only been in the most recent years, with over 1 million prisoners, that the ratio of prisoners to crimes has reached its 1961 level once again. This is a point also made by the American economist Morgan Reynolds, who has used a measure of the 'risk of imprisonment' to demonstrate that the expected punishment for committing any one crime in 1986, after ten years of a steeply rising prison population, was still only 19 days – about one-fifth of the 93 days that an offender could expect as punishment in 1959 (Reynolds, 1991). The key lesson that Murray draws from this is that it is easy to maintain a low crime rate and a high risk of imprisonment, but it is difficult to try to re-establish a high rate of imprisonment after crime has been allowed to get out of hand.

Second, is the lesson drawn by Murray from the American statistics that prison *can* stop a rising crime rate and then begin to reduce it. In this respect he has pointed to the way in which, with a few exceptions, rates for the various serious crimes have been retreating since 1980 when imprisonment rates began to increase.

> As of 1995, property crime is back at the rate it first reached in 1975, with burglary down by more than 40 per cent from its peak. The homicide rate is lower than it has been since 1969. Robbery has bobbed up and down within a narrow range for twenty years. In 1995 it stood at the rate it first reached in 1975. Only one major type of violent crime, aggravated assault (roughly comparable to England's 'wounding'), is still near its peak, and even aggravated assault has been dropping for the last three years.
>
> (Murray, 1997, p. 17)

Murray's arguments have also been supported by other academics, including the economist Stephen Levitt, who has analysed the effectiveness of imprisonment on curbing criminal behaviour. Levitt (1996) calculated that a 1,000 in-mate increase in the prison population in the USA prevented about 4 murders, 53 rapes, 1,200 assaults, 1,100 robberies, 2,600 burglaries and 9,200 larcenies. The summary of the trade-off was computed to be about fifteen crimes saved for the cost of imprisoning one criminal, which Levitt suggested to be cost-effective by almost any measure of the costs of crime (Levitt, 1996).

Langan (1991), a statistician at the Bureau of Justice Statistics, undertook a similar calculation and estimated a rather larger saving in crime from imprisonment (an average of twenty-one crimes saved for every custodial sentence) and estimated that the increase in the US prison population that occurred between 1975 and 1989 probably reduced violent crime by between 10 and 15 per cent (or by about 390,000 crimes).

Against these computations and the conclusion drawn from them that 'prison works' are the doubts of many criminologists about the validity of Murray's arguments. Rutherford (1997), for example, has questioned them on the grounds that the conclusions do not fit the data presented and that they appear to reflect more Murray's ideological standpoint on the role and nature of the State. 'He is an advocate of dismantling public welfare services and a harsh criminal justice system is a necessary permanent accompaniment' (Rutherford, 1997, p. 48). On the other hand Young has criticised the oversimplification of the analysis, and particularly Murray's assertion of 'cause and effect':

> The social world is a complex interactive entity in which any particular social intervention can only possibly have a limited effect on other social events and where the calculation of the effect is always difficult. ... Thus the crime rate is affected by a large number of things; by the level of deterrence exerted by the criminal justice system, to be sure, but also by the levels of informal control in the community, by patterns of employment, by types of child-rearing, by the cultural, political and moral climate, by the level of organised crime, by the patterns of illicit drug use, etc. etc. And to merely add together all these factors is complicated enough but insufficient for it does not allow for human assessment and reflexivity – the *perceived* injustice of unemployment, for instance, or the *felt* injustice of bad policing or imprisonment.
>
> (Young, 1997, p. 33)

The result, according to Young, is strange and distinctly unclear relationships; low rates of imprisonment can act as an effective deterrent when the community is in accord as to the venality of the crime and the impartiality of the criminal justice system. In contrast, high rates of imprisonment can be counterproductive where they are seen as grossly unfair with regard to the level of gravity of the offence and the degree to which the system focuses on particular sections of the community.

Critics of Murray's arguments have also pointed out that the analyses have been based on a period of time (1960s–1990s) in which immense social changes were taking place in patterns of employment, in family structures and in the role of women, with youth culture flourishing, with the illicit use of drugs spreading, with many previously strongly knit communities disintegrating, with the role of the welfare state changing and an underclass of structurally unemployed emerging. In such turbulent times, how could one reasonably suggest that more use of imprisonment would automatically stem the upward trend in crime? In any case, other statistics reveal contradictory patterns. Young (1997), for instance, has commented on Denmark's very low rate of incarceration and yet also low crime rate (compared with the USA where a high use of custody accompanies a very high crime rate). He has also pointed out that although the overall crime rate in the USA declined in recent years, the rate for violent crime, especially for homicide, had only levelled.

If there is any truth in Murray's assertion about the effect of the imprisonment rate on the crime rate, it would require an incredible number of incarcerations to bring crime down to European levels. ... To attempt to learn crime control from the US is rather like travelling to Saudi Arabia to learn about women's rights.

Young, 1997, p. 39)

Above all, critics have questioned what they assert amounts to an accountant's view of criminal justice, where the key performance indicator is not justice but price, not stability of civil society but the cost of exclusion from it and the benefit to those who remain within it.

1.5 Summary

During the early 1990s a renewed polemic developed in the UK around the paradigms of welfare and justice and about the nature and purpose of criminal justice. This debate provides the backcloth to this volume. It has been a debate which has increasingly engaged the attention of politicians, media and the public as well as criminologists and criminal justice practitioners. The book has been written at a formative time in terms of the development of criminal justice policy, shortly after the election of a new Labour government. In many respects, the picture of what had been occurring in criminal justice over the past twenty years or so has proved unclear and inconsistent, having been marked by disjuncture in underlying values and philosophies and by rapid change in terms of legislation and the policy framework. Perhaps that was inevitable in the modern world of fast-developing social, economic and technological realities. Certainly in the same period, and under the same Conservative government, economic management underwent some similarly dramatic shifts in direction as the economy moved successively between recession and boom. Moreover, whatever the perspectives of Chancellors of the Exchequer in their approach to the domestic economy, economic management had long been characterised by shifts in thinking and was increasingly subject to the influence of external factors in an increasingly global economy (Hutton, 1995). In many respects the same might be said of law and order and of criminal justice policy.

However, politics (with a large 'P') and associated shifting ideologies represents just one of the forces underlying change in criminal justice. The central thesis of this volume is that four different dynamics have influenced and shaped contemporary policy and practice in criminal justice: *politics* (Chapter 2), *managerialism* (Chapter 3), *administrative processing* (Chapter 4) and *public voice and participation* (Chapter 5). In the succeeding four chapters, each of these is examined in turn to highlight the traits and legacies and to provide a platform from which to consider the future for criminal justice.

CHAPTER TWO

The politicisation of criminal justice

2.1 Introduction

Since the keeping of law and order has consistently been a function of the Western European nation state, criminal justice has always been a political issue. What was different about the politics of criminal justice in the 1980s and 1990s was, first, the emergence of a different relationship and set of expectations – indeed a different 'contract' – between government and its electorate, and, second, the presentation of 'Law and Order' as a political issue in a manner that changed the criminal justice agenda and in so doing made it available and responsive to public discourse. The outcome was that, by the mid-1990s, there was no going back to the post-war welfare consensus on criminal justice.

This chapter identifies and discusses the implications of three major shifts in the 'contract' between state and citizen, namely, what the contract covers, who is involved, and how the contract is implemented. The chapter then considers how the revised contract played into a changed agenda for criminal justice supported by a shift in the attitude of the public towards crime, by changes in the ways in which government pursued its role in relation to the criminal justice agencies and by the emergence of new criminological theory. Fuelled by a series of notorious criminal justice cases and the public construction placed upon them, the chapter argues that these changes begin to explain why some concerns surfaced as part of the new agenda (for example, victims, prisons) and crucially not others (notably defendants' rights). The chapter ends with a number of observations on the ideology of the new politics of criminal justice and on how that ideology has set a context in the UK consistent with a tough stance on law and order (see Section 1.4).

2.2 The changing role of the state in criminal justice

Historically, the contract between citizens and the state (as represented by the monarchy and Parliament in this country), as elsewhere in Western Europe, has been based on reciprocity. Thus, one of the conditions of subject dependence and of government being permitted to govern, is that the state is accountable for security of the nation's boundaries, security of personal property and personal safety in return for allegiance. That accountability is mobilised through Parliament but remains symbolically with the Head of State. The annual opening of Parliament and the debarring of Black Rod is in recognition of this responsibility. While historically the mutual benefit of state protection and subject dependence were related to conditions of war, including civil war, the same relationship has translated into circumstances of peace such that the public has grown to expect their Government to take responsibility for law and order. When this has not occurred, or indeed when it has occurred only intermittently or where either partner has failed to agree, the contract between the people and the state has been called into question as, indeed, in Northern Ireland and in the former Eastern European bloc.

During the 1980s and 1990s, the contract between people and state in the UK underwent change in three significant respects. First there was an unmistakable shift in what the contract covered; that is, in its locus of control and its content. Using relevant political speeches of the day, David Garland has catalogued the then Conservative Prime Minister and Home Secretary moving the Government's agenda from 'law and order' to one of 'managing crime' (Garland, 1996).

> A primary responsibility of any government at home is to take action to protect people from crime . . . *the guarantee of law and order* (original emphases) is essential to the British Way of Life.
> Speech by John Major, 9 September 1994.
>
> (Quoted by Garland, 1996)

This was all the more remarkable since

> by the mid-twentieth century, the state was promising not just to punish legal violations, and quell internal unrest but actually to

govern in ways which would curb or cure the social problem of crime.

(Garland, 1996, p. 449)

According to Garland, the inconsistency of 'government-speak' during the 1970s and 1980s amounted to backing-off from over-optimistic claims originally made about tackling law and order in the face of a rising tide of dissatisfaction among the electorate and against the background of slim majorities in the House of Commons.

The second shift in the 'contract' concerned those with whom it was made. The post-war welfare consensus had been built out of a Fabian-style triumvirate of authority of church, state and legislature. The triumvirate had 'contracted' implicitly and explicitly with the individual, the family and the community (those basic building blocks of post-war sociology) to build a 'welfare society'. The result was a set of expectations and understandings which, if not universally shared, was widely acknowledged, bolstered by a residual class system, by the institutions of school, marriage, gender and the workplace, and by tacit acceptance of inequality and threat of the consequences of economic depression.

The social changes of the 1950s, 1960s and 1970s to women, families, the workplace and communities, which became explicit in the 1980s and 1990s, effectively dismantled the fabric and culture which supported the welfare consensus (James, 1994). For many, the authority that had long been vested in the church had increasingly come to be seen as irrelevant. The judiciary had become subject to much cynicism and criticism on account of its élitism and the credibility of the courts threatened by a series of misplaced judgements. Moreover, the unity of the state was called into question, for example, with Scotland and Northern Ireland pressing nationalist, and Brussels pressing sovereignty, concerns. Neither the infrastructure nor the culture sustaining the old welfare consensus remained.

That which replaced it was the infrastructure and the culture of 'the market'. The market ousted the triumvirate of the welfare consensus, replacing it with a new pattern of arms-length agencies (for example, the Prison Service Agency) and with a mixed economy of commissioners and providers of service involving public, private and voluntary sectors.

How this process was implemented marks the third major shift in the 'contract'. Instead of making policy through recognised institutions within a climate of agreement and with the support of key professional bodies and academics, the Government sought to deliver through the medium of management (see Chapter 3).

While there were clear financial imperatives behind the mixed economy (James, 1994) in choosing to emphasise management as the medium, the Government also chose to downplay the policy advice function of its top civil servants and the findings of academic research, even from within its own domain, the Research and Planning Unit of the Home Office. In choosing to pursue what might have been regarded as the 'business case' for central control and to encourage the mechanisms of the market into public services (Walsh, 1995), the Government also chose by default to ignore the wider case for social justice previously represented by the church and often by the judiciary. Indeed, criticisms from church leaders about new proposals from the Government, or about the general thrust of criminal justice policy, were invariably seen by ministers of state as meddling in politics and generally invoked a sharp response. Together with several instances of very public disagreement between members of the senior judiciary and the Home Secretary, this reinforced the marginalisation of both church and judiciary from policy-making, thereby facilitating an increasingly narrow field of vision and set of responsibilities for government.

The effect of a mixed economy during the 1980s was to create a new interface between the state and its public in the form of a number of new criminal justice agencies, often with short-term funding and operating on a project basis. It was the multiplicity of such agencies, together with the perceived inefficiencies of the statutory criminal justice agencies, that prompted and encouraged the systematising of the process consistent with the management ethos of efficiency and effectiveness (Audit Commission, 1996).

This represented an agenda quite removed from traditional notions of governmental responsibility for civil society and for public protection. Indeed what we find by the mid-1990s is government, far from capturing and owning these notions, actively 'exporting' responsibility for public safety and protection to communities. This was apparent both in ministerial exhortations to car and home owners to take greater care to protect their property and in the promotion of Neighbourhood Watch schemes, support for Safer Cities Projects and other local partnership-based crime prevention schemes. This was a considerable turnaround on the traditional contract between governor and governed.

2.3 Redefining the criminal justice agenda

The political agenda which had emerged by the late 1990s had become dominated by a number of very specific concerns, including prison sentencing, victims, drugs, youth crime including street and car crime, sex offending and violence by mentally disordered offenders in the community. While it was necessary for the agenda of politicians to demonstrate responsiveness to those aspects of law and order and criminal justice that had come to public prominence, the question is: 'Why did politicians choose to acknowledge, rather than downplay these problems?' Indeed, why did Michael Howard, as Home Secretary, add to public anxieties by his fervent commitment to a 'war' against criminal behaviour and draw attention to statistics and trends which risked undermining the traditional reputation of the Conservative Party as the Party of Law and Order?

The answer is that, while these problems were important in themselves, they surfaced as concerns partly because of the deeper and emergent changes which they represented. The first concern was a clear shift in the attitude of the public towards crime, which the Government simply could not afford to ignore. The second was the changed stance within Government in relation to its role with criminal justice agencies. The third was the effect of new criminological theory. These three factors were interrelated and self-reinforcing. They were driven in a particular political direction by a series of serious and publicly discussed crimes such as the murders of the infant James Bulger and headteacher Patrick Lawrence. The result was to create a context sympathetic to the tough stance on crime simultaneously unfolding in the USA (Murray, 1997).

2.4 Public attitude to crime

The apparent shift in public attitude towards crime was based, first, on the public *experience* of the reality of crime; second, on the loss of public confidence in existing agencies, approaches and mechanisms to resolve the problem of crime; and third, on self-reinforcing public perception of the scale of crime and the risks of being victimised.

Any understanding of the shift in criminal justice policy in the late twentieth century has to begin from, or take into account very seriously, the public experience of the reality of crime as it invaded and pervaded everyday life at a level increasingly perceived as unacceptable. Official statistics might report a fall in recorded crime, and present figures to demonstrate that more police officers were now on the streets. However, the public had other benchmarks from which to draw conclusions about the state of law and order. For some it was more likely to be the known reality of the availability of drugs in schools or the prevalence of unsolicited begging and harassment on the streets, or the almost predictable incidence of car crime, burglary and pickpocketing in urban environments. The failure of the 'welfare lobby' within criminal justice to acknowledge the significance of these realities, to impute it to tabloid manipulation, and to persist instead in trying to argue the case for sympathy and understanding for the predicament of offenders, only served to undermine credibility gained in the past. From the public's point of view the welfare approach to crime had palpably failed. The Home Secretary's promise to the Conservative Party Conference and to the wider public in 1993, that he would 'get tough on crime' (as reported in *The Independent*, 18 October 1993), had a resonance with the mood of the majority. It made sense within the public experience.

It also made sense in the public imagination. Important in the construction of that imagination was a series of notorious events that were to shake public confidence in law and order, in the justice dispensed in the courts, and in the capacity of Government to carry out its manifesto commitments. The events included prison riots and break-outs, the overturning of convictions for IRA bombings, the Dunblane massacre, and a succession of public inquiries in respect of murders by mentally ill persons in the community.

The significance of these events was not simply that they happened, but the interpretation that was placed upon them. They were seen as symptoms of a far greater malaise and reinforced much deeper fear of endemic lawlessness. They connected with the range of personal experiences of having been a victim of (petty) crime and played into personal fears of attack and a deep sense of insecurity. This fear was often combined with an obsessive fascination for violent and salacious crime as evidenced in press coverage of the murders at Cromwell Street, Gloucester, and of the subsequent trial of Rosemary West. Important also in the construction of the public imagination was television's treatment of crime. In

1996, for the first time, serious crime appeared in family soap operas shown, at peak viewing time, with a murder in Brookside. It became increasingly difficult to separate fact from fiction with the reconstruction of real crime, for example, in the television series Crime Watch, UK.

Such voyeuristic appeal arguably relies upon the disconnectedness of crime and the criminal from the actions and behaviours of the rest of us. Only by distancing ourselves from crime might we adopt and sustain pejorative notions towards those we describe as criminal. Defining actions as criminal thus serves to reaffirm the rightness of our own values and ways of life. It is therefore partly a way of managing our own personal and deep insecurities of identity and status and our need for control over our own lives. Violent crime, because of its perceived arbitrariness and unpredictability, confronts us with these concerns as potential victims in a particularly dramatic way ('there, but for the grace of God, go I'). When held by a critical mass, these deep personal fears can be exacerbated into hysterical reactions (Campbell, 1993). In such circumstances the call for punishment becomes part of a need to see order restored and the leviathan of disorder and lawlessness overcome.

2.5 The role of government

Important to the public change of attitude to crime were the changes of role within government itself, as represented by the concerns of successive Home Secretaries. A series of reductions can be traced in the emphasis given to their responsibilities. A broad commitment to maintaining 'law and order' gave way to a focus on criminal justice as provided by criminal justice agencies. This facilitated a narrowing emphasis on managing crime, which, because of government market-style reforms, increasingly amounted to managing punishment (Home Office, 1990). By the mid-1990s this had reduced to a preoccupation with sentencing. This series of reductions was consistent with the ideology and practice of the market as promoted throughout the public sector in the Thatcher and post-Thatcher era (see Chapter 4). At a superficial level here was something of a paradox. For while the Government was indeed demonstrating more assertiveness and determination to achieve its purposes, the impact of its involvement was simultaneously and steadily reducing.

In the new mixed economy, government was left with primarily a managerial function to perform. This managerial function was interpreted in a particular way, consistent with the particular interpretation of management common across government at the time. So the role of government (in criminal justice, as in social care, health, education and other public services) was reduced to one of trying to set up and manage the market within specific services (Harden, 1992).

Setting up the market meant regulating the contributions of existing participants in the criminal justice process in order to create a level playing field, stimulating independent provision through incentives and managing what became known as stakeholders in criminal justice. This process goes some way to explain the fortunes of the judiciary as it sought to maintain its primacy (in the triumvirate with church and state) rather than the stakeholder status allocated to it by the marketplace. Managing the market meant setting up competition, managing it through tendering and benchmarking processes (among others) and then evaluating achievement against predetermined performance targets. The rolling privatisation of the Prison Service through agency status and regulation, followed by tendering for private prisons, provides an example of government acting out a managerial function.

The new, limited role of government had its costs as well as its benefits in the Home Office. Together with the exporting of services went the exporting of concerns and solutions. This worked well in the absence of any strong direction on policy. It became a problem, however, when the Home Secretary wished to pursue a hard line on offending behaviour without the means to do so. In giving away accountability and responsibility for policy, the Home Secretary found, to his cost, that he had given away substantial authority. This, too, had happened in the Health Service with the creation of the National Health Service Executive (NHSE) run by career managers. It was rather more serious for the Home Office, however, for in giving away authority and policy, government arguably gave away its legitimacy based on its primary function to deliver social order. Indeed, the behaviour of the Home Secretary, Michael Howard, during the 1990s, perceived as erratic, was possibly induced by the need to recover legitimacy and primary authority while under pressure to pursue what rapidly came to be perceived as an unsuccessful market in criminal justice (see Chapter 4). This would explain a series of individual public humiliations and punishments administered by the Home Secretary and designed to demonstrate a government tough on crime but able now only to deliver in the limited area of punishment and sentencing, and then only by wresting power away from the judiciary, for example, in the non-release of Myra Hindley.

It also explains why the parliamentary stages of the Crime (Sentences) Bill 1997 became a battleground between the Home Secretary and the judiciary. Here, the traditionally healthy tension between elected representatives and professional officers over policy decisions became distorted by the Home Secretary's challenge, first, to the legitimacy of the judiciary to express opinion and, second, to the extent of their discretion in sentencing. Winning this battle was important to a Home Secretary who, by this time, was preoccupied by sentencing as one of the few areas of authority still within his grasp (Penal Affairs Consortium, 1997).

David Garland, drawing on Foucault's commentary on public executions during the French Revolution, offers a less generous explanation of the Government's obsession with punishment and sentencing.

> A show of punitive force against individuals is used to repress any acknowledgement of the state's inability to control crime to acceptable levels. A willingness to deliver harsh punishments to convicted offenders magically compensates a failure to deliver security to the public at large. (Garland, 1996, p. 460)

2.6 New criminological theory

The third factor which underlay the new politics of criminal justice concerned the new theories of criminology. The welfare consensus had powerfully united psychological, sociological and structural/political theories of the causes of crime of the 1950s, 1960s and 1970s, which together argued that criminal behaviour on the part of individuals was a product of broader social problems rising out of personal inadequacy (low self-esteem or achievement), social upbringing (family and peer culture) and structural disadvantage (poverty, homelessness, unemployment). Responses were focused on the twin activities of addressing the behaviour of individual offenders and community development. The assumption was that, because everyone was considered capable of personal reform and of rehabilitation in the community, crime would reduce as personal inadequacies and structural inequalities were addressed.

The new criminologies focused not on individual criminal personalities but on criminal events. The spirit of the new thinking was that, in committing crime, offenders were exercising deliberate choices and taking calculated risks, the outcomes of which were known and predictable. It attributed to the offenders an instrumental view of their criminal acts, based on opportunity cost and personal decision. This pragmatic view focused on 'cause and effect', whereby a given offence automatically attracted a given penalty. This contrasted with previous concern with the wider issues of social justice. It promoted a preoccupation with penalties. For this reason there emerged a new strand of research and development concerning the econometrics of crime, sentencing, victimology and the measurement of effectiveness of different penalties.

In this new scenario crime came to be 'managed', not so much by working with offenders and addressing the social situations in which crime was seen to flourish as by addressing the circumstances of the particular criminal event. This meant, for example, encouraging the use of credit cards instead of cash, introducing video cameras in schools and shopping areas, targeting known persistent offenders and assessing risk to the community of releasing prisoners on parole. It gave rise to a particular interpretation of victimology, whereby the victims were used as part of the law enforcement process in criminal justice rather than addressing their own needs. This is not to underestimate the value of supporting work undertaken with victims (Rock, 1990). On the contrary, it is to reinforce that victims need to be part of the criminal justice agenda because of who they are in their own right, and should not be used as part of the way the state chooses to deal with offenders (see Chapter 5). In the same way sentencing needs to be seen within the context of the whole criminal justice process, not as part of a preoccupation with penalties or as a demonstration of a government 'tough on crime'.

Arguably both the new and the old criminologies have much to offer, not least together. It is said that every theory has its day. The social problem orientation of the welfarists fitted well with a generation of social workers, teachers and youth workers excited by the new subjects of psychology, sociology and politics in the booming welfare economy of the 1960s, some of whom by the 1980s and 1990s had progressed in career terms to occupy very senior and influential positions. The new criminologies fit much more successfully with a market economy where criminal events are separated from offenders and their situations and where the cost and value of intervention can be evaluated. In this sense theory is both a product and a cameo of its time.

2.7 Conclusion: politics and ideology

This chapter has identified and reviewed the contract between the state and its people and discussed the implications of changes in that contract for criminal justice. The chapter has gone on to consider the pressures behind a changing agenda in criminal justice. We close with consideration of the ways in which criminal justice, during the period under review, contributed to the development of a revised political ideology – an ideology that made a return to the welfarist position unrealistic in the foreseeable future, and one that set a context conducive to a tough line on crime (Murray, 1997).

First, revising the contract between people and the state helped to change the remit and intervention of criminal justice from a comprehensive social policy (of which law and order was only one part) to a project-based interventionist approach to tackling identified problems (for example, drugs and/or car crime).

Second, this in turn represented a shift in ideology from patriarchy to pluralism. This was a shift from an assumed or explicit collectivist responsibility for a safe society, delivered by a benevolent, if patriarchal, government to a model where central resources were allocated to particular issues according to multiple pressures often with only token accommodation to manifesto or policy commitments. The centralist consensus in the UK was based on 'Rowntree's Five Giants' (Rowntree, 1902), which underpinned the social policy of the early twentieth century, and that of the welfare consensus of the Beveridge reforms.

Third, the adoption of a pluralist model marks a break with Western European political practice in favour of a system appropriate to a federal government arrangement, such as the USA and Australia, where the imposition of centralism has proved impossible (for example, Clinton's Health Reforms in the USA), and where there is no lengthy tradition of a social policy and social ethic which serves to bind the interests of disparate communities and states, as there is, by exception, in Canada.

29

LIVERPOOL JOHN MOORES UNIVERSITY
LEARNING SERVICES

Fourth, of course, the pluralist model fits much more comfortably with the introduction of the market mechanism because it has within it a way of handling competition and a rationale for inequity. Thus the role of government is reduced in pluralism to managing competing interests, supposedly within the framework of a publicly accepted manifesto.

Fifth, the unintended consequence of the market mechanism introduced into public service was to generate uncertainty at all levels in the system. Market testing, privatisation, agency status and competitive tendering, were all methods by which the state sought to manage an uncertain world, but did so only by passing on some of the risk to independent, voluntary sector and quasi-governmental institutions in the medium term. In turn, these institutions eventually passed on the risk to service users. At every level people felt trapped by this process – a process of imposition, which created an unintended effect of dispensing punishment on those least able to resist it (Marris, 1996) and imposing vulnerability on the most vulnerable.

Sixth, and finally, it is the disaggregation of the state from social policy to intervention within a series of agreed and budgeted concerns and the replacement of collective responsibility with the instrumentalism of the market which, combined with a very real and deep fear of crime and loss of certainty, generates the conditions under which both government and the public become eager participants in a tough stance on crime.

CHAPTER THREE

Managerialism and criminal justice

3.1 Introduction

This chapter argues that managerialism, first introduced into public services from the early 1980s, was a key dynamic in the shaping of criminal justice in the period under review. Managerialism refers to the implementation of a variety of techniques, generally borrowed from the private sector within a culture of cost efficiency and service effectiveness. It is here distinguished from management in the traditional sense, a broader concept which refers to the balancing and direction of resources to achieve certain intents, for it is argued that management, as first introduced into UK public services under the Thatcher Government, was a specific kind of management, here identified as managerialism. This was not only a UK phenomenon, although Margaret Thatcher and her Government certainly gave a particular spin to its interpretation and impetus to its development.

The chapter outlines the key features of managerialism as it affected criminal justice agencies and assesses its overall impact on the shape of criminal justice towards the end of the 1990s. It begins by setting the framework of the reforms.

The significance of management in the period of the reforms had its roots in an earlier and much broader international initiative. As early as 1945, Daniel Bell had identified what he called 'a management revolution' sweeping across Western Europe and the USA, a revolution as significant in his eyes as the industrial revolution a century earlier (Bell, 1974). His ideas were echoed by Foucault (1986) who foresaw what they described as the end of an era as Western countries shifted increasingly from manufacturing-based to service-based economies. For while production units needed controllers and supervisors, services needed managing.

Post-war public services in the UK had been largely created and designed according to the manufacturing model of production that was dominant at the time. It was a model that was effective enough in 'producing' hospitals, schools, houses and residential homes, which were products of the public service assembly line. It was not a good model for creating services which needed to be flexible and responsive to the needs of the service user and the preferences of citizens in general. According to the manufacturing production model, public services were delivered by means of bureaucracies, centralised units designed to deliver reliable consistency and line management accountability across a range of standard products, because reliability, consistency, standardisation and accountability from public services were badly needed after the war. To all intents and purposes the bureaucracy was the assembly line equivalent of the manufacturing production factory, with clear lines of command, job and task specification, highly segmented structure and authority attached to role seniority (James, 1994). And bureaucracies were run not by managers but by administrators, whose task it was to ensure the flow of information from top to bottom and its co-ordination. Bureaucracies were consequently particularly appropriate vehicles for the delivery of state services (viz. Eastern bloc countries) (Foster and Plowden, 1996).

During the 1960s, public services became subject to wide-scale planning techniques, as new towns and new infrastructures were built. Management concepts were beginning to find their way into public service. Of particular significance was Drucker's concept of 'management by objectives' (Drucker, 1954), a rational business model which seemed to fit well with planning for the future. This model and its derivatives were embraced by the newly emerging business schools which were promoting management as a discipline of its own. In the succeeding years, and in the light of developments in information technology, communications and mobility, the potential grew for alternative ways of working based on decentralised units and delegation of authority.

It was against this context that Margaret Thatcher assumed her premiership in the UK. The immediate challenge she set herself was to control what she regarded as runaway public expenditure and to contain the enhanced demand for service which public service bureaucracies had in part helped to create. In this project she was in close alignment with the objectives being pursued across the Western world, but most particularly in the USA, where President Reagan and his administration's strongly monetarist policies had special appeal (Osborne and Gaebler, 1992). In part drawing on the principles of the US tradition of a more limited public sector, and in part on the ideas of the New Right think tanks on this side of the Atlantic, Mrs Thatcher's project in the UK developed a particular political and ideological perspective which embraced free market principles. She perceived public services, with their bureaucratic tendencies, as inherently inefficient and the professionals working within them as self-serving. The answer, she believed, was very simple. Public services should be run as businesses (Clarke et al., 1994).

In this respect, her initiative was strongly reinforced by a number of business-minded ministers, such as Ken Clarke, Michael Heseltine and Nicholas Ridley. They quickly perceived that if public services were to operate as businesses they required (1) a market to operate within, (2) competition within that market and (3) the presence of consumers. The story of the managerial reforms reflected in part the placement of such ministers among Whitehall departments. The initial momentum for the reforms in education and health, for example, was directly attributable to the presence of Ken Clarke. It reflected also public services being picked off according to their size of budget and ease of pickings (James, 1994). For these reasons criminal justice services were only marginally and intermittently affected by managerial reform and the new business culture. The marginality and inconsistency of implementation itself raised distinctive problems.

3.2 Managerialism in criminal justice

The Thatcher reforms of public services have been extensively described and evaluated elsewhere and the arguments are not reproduced here (see, for example, Pollitt, 1990; Hood, 1991; Dunleavy, 1994; Raine and Willson, 1993; James, 1994; Newman and Clarke, 1994). While they were ideologically driven, in practice and on reflection they centred around the pragmatics of cost efficiency and demonstrable service effectiveness. Cost efficiency, captured in the euphemism of 'value for money', challenged traditional assumptions and approaches in budget making and service administration. Previously, budgets were mostly calculated on the basis of past provision rather than on identified need; services allocated on the basis of universal distribution, means-tests or the exercise of professional discretion rather than according to costs or demand.

Demonstrable service effectiveness was achieved through a set of revised and transparent accountability processes which overtook traditional professional accountabilities for practice and a generalised, if well intentioned, public service ethic. Performance management techniques were increasingly employed to measure achievement at individual, agency and service levels against predetermined targets and priorities, an application that was very different from the traditional bureaucratic processing of referrals in response to direct demand.

The reforms impacted on criminal justice in the four distinct areas of organisational design and development, agency function, efficiency and productivity, and staffing.

3.3 Organisational design and development

As indicated, criminal justice agencies were never subjected to the large-scale structural reforms of, for example, the health service. For one thing, reform was politically very difficult not least because the doctrine of the separation of powers gave independence to the judiciary. For another, the agencies were themselves dispersed, and unco-ordinated, unlike in health, a national health service, where the central administration could be quickly and easily targeted. In any case, the Thatcher Government placed higher priority in terms of organisational reform upon other public services, notably those covered by local government (including education) and in the health sector. Somewhat behind other public services, the criminal justice agencies were put under pressure – first through exhortation and eventually by financial controls and performance monitoring – to become more efficient and effective. It is possible that a fuller managerialist agenda of market-style reforms would have eventually come to criminal justice under the Conservatives. As it happened, however, the reform agenda at the Home Office took a rather different path with the arrival of the last in the line of Conservative Home Secretaries, Michael Howard, and focused instead on the policy agenda of getting tough on crime (see Chapter 2). As a result, the main emphasis of managerialism for criminal justice agencies remained at the level of trying to meet the performance targets that were demanded of them by government while also coping with increasingly tight budgets.

Against this general picture, however, there were some important, though isolated, examples of a more developed managerialist agenda in relation to organisational design. The Prison Service, in particular, felt the pressure of the market through the tendering and contracting of some jails (initially those newly commissioned). The award of contracts to private security firms to undertake prisoner escort duties (between prisons and courts) was another significant example. There was also the hiving off from the Home Office and Lord Chancellor's Department respectively of the operation of the prisons and the administration of the Crown Court and County Court, through the establishment of 'Next Steps' agencies in the form of the Prison Service Agency and the Court Service Agency. A similar organisational model was proposed for the magistrates' courts (Home Office, 1989) although this was successfully resisted by the concerted efforts of magistrates and their clerks. Indeed, strong opposition from powerful groups within criminal justice, notably the judiciary and chief constables, was a major factor in limiting the extent of the managerialist market-style reforms. Another constraint was the dearth of alternative providers in the market. The reality in relation to prisons and prisoner escorts, for example, was that there were only a very few firms in the UK which were in a position to bid for contracts, which meant that they were immediately in a preferred partner status, and an obstacle to the entry into the market of new firms. The 'five per cent rule' of contracting that was applied to the Probation Service was similarly unambitious when compared with the regime of compulsory competitive tendering (CCT) imposed on local government, although it was sufficient to reinforce progressive internal changes within some probation areas. Other opportunities for market-style reforms were simply not taken, reflecting not only the political difficulties associated with criminal justice, but also the instincts and priorities of the particular ministers in post and the signals thus given to their civil servants. The Home Office review of the organisation of magistrates' courts conducted in 1989, for instance, created an opportunity to contract out the administration of the lower courts, either on a national basis to a single firm, or, as had been the normal practice across the country in earlier times, to firms of locally practising solicitors, who undertook the functions of advising the local justices and administering their courts alongside their private practices. However, in the event, these options were hardly considered and the debate simply centred on whether in-house court administration should be nationalised or left under the control of local magistrates' courts committees.

The creation of quasi-markets in health and social care had led, in the second stage of the reforms, to significant attempts at market repositioning as providers struggled to get ahead in the race to win contracts. The result was a series of mergers and alliances based on horizontal and vertical integration of services such that purchasers could buy according to their preferred choice. Because there was no equivalent scale of market in criminal justice, there was no significant leverage on agencies to change their behaviour or practices except at the margins and, even then, largely because of internal motivation (though because of uncertainty about their future, the agencies felt under pressure). The result was that government felt it necessary to intervene artificially to restructure in pursuit of efficiency and effectiveness gains presumed elsewhere to flow from the market approach. Amalgamation proposals were announced for magistrates' courts, police and probation services. In the case of magistrates' courts, the Lord Chancellor proposed a reduction in the number of local magistrates' courts areas from 105 to between 50 and 60 in the 1992 White Paper, *A New Framework for Local Justice* (Lord Chancellor's Department, 1992). The Government also gave consideration to the idea of a single national police force as well as to mergers of the smaller forces and to reducing the number of probation service areas (Leishman et al., 1996). In the event, none of these proposals was implemented as intended. Indeed, only a handful of mergers took place, and then, only because there was local agreement to the idea. In the main, the Government submitted to the high level of opposition from influential representative bodies (notably the Association of Chief Police Officers, the Police Federation, the Magistrates' Association, the Justices' Clerks' Society, and the Association of Chief Officers of Probation).

More successful were the initiatives on organisational redesign begun within services themselves. To some, it was becoming clear that the traditional ways of working were not going to suit the future. Bureaucracy was not only out of favour, it was also out of date. To others, the threat of Mrs Thatcher's 'iron fist' was sufficient to mobilise internal reform rather than wait for change to be imposed. And others, watching the reforms, saw some useful techniques worth copying in their own services. Organisational structures changed in three main ways: they became less hierarchical, sometimes with whole tiers removed; they became leaner and tighter as jobs widened and staff numbers reduced; and they were driven by managerial rather than professional processes.

This last characteristic was particularly relevant to criminal justice agencies which were largely professional in character. Professional structures begin from an assumption that the professional knows best and that the organisation exists to service that expertise. Then again, it is individualistic in character. Professionals are individually qualified and seek individual resolution with individual clients. In contrast, management structures assume that the best decisions are made at the top and that is why managers are paid more than practitioners. Most public service organisations had run both structures in tandem with finance and support services operating management structures and operations working through professional structures. The effect of reducing hierarchy and making organisations leaner and tighter was to expose the inherent tension between managerial and professional systems. The new status ascribed to the manager meant that, in that tension, professionals felt devalued with their autonomy increasingly challenged by seemingly unnecessary regulations and procedures.

A particular characteristic of the reforms in criminal justice was dissonance between the traditional agencies, for whom the changes all too often came as an unwelcome interference in traditional practice (as for example, in the courts) and those agencies newly established on managerialist principles (notably, the Crown Prosecution Service).

In conclusion, the absence in government of, first, a clear and agreed strategic direction for criminal justice (see Chapter 2) and, second, agreed means of implementation designed for its achievement, led to an inconsistent and patchy series of government interventions. In the absence of innovative and co-ordinated initiatives by agencies to tackle evident shortcomings in how criminal justice was working, the effect on agencies was of general confusion, uncertainty and low morale, particularly among professional groups.

A ready example of all this was to be found in the magistrates' courts, which had been slow to recognise the need for change and generally defensive in response to the Government's call for better management. The consequence was that, following a Home Office review (Home Office, 1989), a revised organisational framework was proposed in a White Paper (Lord Chancellor's Department, 1992), much of which was subsequently implemented under the Police and Magistrates' Courts Act 1994 (Home Office, 1994a). There were two main strands to the new framework. First was the reduction through amalgamations in the number of separate local magistrates' courts areas (discussed above), which generated much opposition among magistrates and staff about the dilution of local identity. Second, a new top tier of managers was introduced, called justices' chief executives, and was imposed above the justices' clerks who had previously been the autonomous heads of profession in their own local court organisations. The aim of this reform, like the amalgamation proposals, was to generate efficiency improvements by cutting out wasteful duplication and by enabling more flexibility in the allocation of resources. The loss of status and authority by the justices' clerks was, however, deeply felt. As a concession to them, the Lord Chancellor agreed that those appointed to the new posts of justices' chief executive would have to have legal qualifications, thereby inviting justices' clerks to apply. In practice, the candidates with management skills and aptitudes were the ones who were appointed. Indeed, to the dismay of the Justices' Clerks' Society, a few appointments were made of lawyers who had not been justices' clerks and/or had no previous experience in magistrates' courts. The consequent low morale of the profession pre-empted much tactical non-co-operation on the part of justices' clerks with their new managers and resulted in protracted disputes over legal authority and discretion. In this respect, the provisions of the Police and Magistrates' Courts Act 1994 offered insufficient clarity. A number of long-serving justices' clerks sought early retirement, which meant a loss of much experience for the courts. Many others accepted redundancy terms in local reorganisation plans that were prompted by budgetary problems (exacerbated by the costs of the new top tier of management).

3.4 Task and function of criminal justice agencies

A key characteristic of traditional bureaucratic services was that they were procedurally driven. That procedure may not always have been written down, but what such agencies did and how they did it was known, bounded and consistent. Indeed, the purpose of staff induction programmes was to introduce new appointees into the administrative constraints and regulations within which the agency operated. A key characteristic of the new and reformed agencies was that they were driven by purpose. That purpose was explicit and often single-minded. Indeed, in its early and rational stages of development, managerialism was driven by an 'ideal' process model of visioning, planning, strategy, implementation, monitoring and review. Government departments required agencies to prepare strategic business plans consistent with their own, to identify priorities and targets and to monitor, review and report on achievement. Again the magistrates' courts provide an example in the form of a new statutory duty placed on the local committees to prepare and update strategic plans on a regular basis, the quality of which became subject to scrutiny by a newly formed Inspectorate.

The possible inappropriateness of rational planning mechanisms to complex environments with multiple stakeholders was unappreciated at the time by the civil servants who dictated the process, as well as by some managers who had been trained in the science, but not the art, of management. The health service experience of being overwhelmed by competing pressures and priorities (for example, in relation to hospital closures) provided a salutary message but, by this time, managerialist techniques were firmly embedded. For some, the criminal justice agencies' failure to get across, or of government to take on board, the complexities of public service functions led to disillusionment and dissatisfaction with the reforms. Others simply worked harder and faster, mistakenly believing that this would in itself resolve what were in fact competing pressures. In this they ran after a rapidly emerging series of new managerial methods and techniques, each of which promised enhanced performance. They included organisational restructuring, changes of leadership, unit business planning, customer service, excellence and total quality initiatives, process reengineering and many more. Any and all of these methods were successful as levers to mobilise change provided support for that change was forthcoming in the first place. They were unsuccessful where they were used not as levers but as solutions in their own right and where support for change was not forthcoming. Where their use was inappropriate in practice it generated initiative fatigue and organisational stress. Increasing pressure was then put on leaders of organisations and agencies to resolve complex problems in seemingly simplistic ways. In this situation the false certainty assumed by some leaders had the appearance of machismo management. This reinforced the image of struggle between the 'caring professionals' and the 'heartless managers' and generated more shroud-waving.

Despite these difficulties, a few managers were able to work with the front-stage rationalist model required by the managerial culture, while practising the backstage non-rational behaviour required of effective management. While managerialism required an explicit and rational strategic planning process up-front, most managers found themselves acting first and making strategy after, simply because change was happening so fast and the environment was unpredictable. For them, management – while it was publicly about visioning, planning, implementing and reviewing practice – was privately about acting (implementing), buying off (reviewing), establishing preferred patterns of action (making strategy) and matching these against long-term intent (vision). Holding front- and backstage activities together proved to be the task of the effective manager.

3.5 Efficiency and productivity

Runaway public expenditure provided its own rationale for public service reform though, again, criminal justice services were not initially exposed to cost savings to the same degree as other public services. Nevertheless, the extent to which the recommendations of the Royal Commission on Criminal Justice (Runciman, 1993) emphasised efficiency and productivity considerations was indicative of the degree to which they had become embedded in criminal justice by the early 1990s (Field and Thomas, 1994).

There were particular sensitivities about cost savings in relation to the pursuit of justice which precluded debate, notably in the courts in relation to sentencing decisions. Efficiency initiatives raised disproportionate anger and opposition within the agencies for whom pressure on budgets went far enough to cause dismay but not far enough to generate significant entrepreneurial alternatives.

The method of reform used to control expenditure and so seek efficiency gains, service by service, followed a well-trodden and unimaginative path already rehearsed in other public services. Cash limits were imposed to put a ceiling on spending. Some funding was ring-fenced to require services to meet government-set priorities. Formulae were adopted to resolve differentials in geographic distribution, and amended in the light of subsequent improved needs analysis and political appeal. Business plans were required to ensure accountability for spending in line with a master business plan for each service created by the Government. Eventually index-linking of cash limits was abandoned and cuts imposed, enforcing efficiency savings and rationing decisions in respect of staffing establishments and the services provided. This process was replicated in the local magistrates' courts, probation and police, as well as in the national services, the Crown Court and the Crown Prosecution Service.

The efficiency requirements had three identified effects. First, most services simply tried to do more with less. In the absence of a clear central strategy or purpose at government level for priority funding across all services, the spirit tended to be parsimonious and negative. It focused on cost-saving and service cuts and low-level processing activities. For example, the magistrates' courts information system (MIS) developed in the mid-1980s by the Home Office, used a set of key indicators (KIs) by which the performance of individual courts could be monitored and compared. Of the four such KIs, one concerned the quality of service, while the other three focused explicitly on efficiency and productivity: average cost per case, delays in case completions, and the level of outstanding fine arrears.

Second, where financial pressures could not be brought to bear on services, productivity improvements were sought in criminal justice processes to address problems of delay and hence indirect costs. An example was a Home Office study of delay (Home Office, 1997). The terms of reference for the study explicitly linked the interests of justice with efficiency and productivity with the purpose of finding 'ways of expediting the progress of cases through the criminal justice system from initiation to resolution, consistent with the interests of justice and securing value for money' (Home Office, 1997, p. 1).

In various respects the report offered a contentious remedy to the problem of delay; in each case making proposals which gave priority to efficiency gains in addition to the traditional views of the interests of justice. For example, the report argued that a critical problem lay in the locational separation (and consequential inefficiency) of the police (the investigators) and the Crown Prosecution Service (the prosecutors). The report recommended the accommodation of prosecutors at each main police station to ensure faster responses; also that, in 'guilty plea' cases, prosecutors should work from 'abbreviated files' (rather than from full case files) thus saving police preparation time. In addition, the report proposed the deployment of non-lawyers by the Crown Prosecution Service (CPS) to review files for simpler cases and to prosecute them in court, again to avoid delays caused by the scarcity of CPS lawyers and to reduce costs.

The report also argued for changes in the procedural arrangements in magistrates' courts at the pre-trial stage, in particular, advocating the extension of powers – traditionally those of the judiciary alone – to their legal advisers, the magistrates' clerks. The argument was that a case should only be put before magistrates when it was ready to proceed. The recommendation was controversial in presenting pre-trial decision-making as 'administrative' and therefore not the business of the court.

At the same time, the report argued for change in the jurisdictional boundaries between the magistrates' court and the Crown Court and for the abandonment of the defendant's right to elect jury trial in 'either way' cases. Instead, the report proposed that all the more serious cases should *start* in the Crown Court (rather than be transferred from the magistrates' court) and that the magistrates, not the defendant, should decide in 'either way' cases whether or not the case should be heard at the Crown Court. While resolving a problem of delay and potential abuse by some defendants, this meant that all defendants would effectively be barred from exercising choice about their trial, and only at the discretion of magistrates could they obtain access to jury trial and to supervision of the case by a professional judge.

The third effect of the efficiency requirements was that they had the effect of stimulating some innovation, although this remained at the level of individual rather than service initiative. For example, caught between 80 per cent Home Office and 20 per cent local authority funding – both under pressure – some individual Chief Officers of Probation began to look elsewhere for funding within their local com- munities. This included creating some innovative joint work with health services on drugs, suicides and mental disorder (Home Office and Department of Health, 1996) and Single Regeneration Budget bids on community safety in partnership with other community agencies.

3.6 Staffing

The process of organisational redesign, clarification of agency task and function, and of enhancing efficiency and productivity all had major implications for staffing. Efficiency savings combined with stricter definition of core services and organisational redesign meant that in some cases whole levels of service hierarchies were removed. For example, some Probation Services replaced both Assistant Chief Probation Officers and Senior Probation Officers with a single tier of Unit Managers. This put pressure on those who remained to deliver high performance against previously determined performance management criteria.

Again criminal justice services paid a high price for their reluctance to take the initiative in implementing their own reforms. Inconsistent and piecemeal implementation meant that the implications for staff were inadequately confronted. Elsewhere in public services, concerns over staffing were more comprehensively addressed by deliberate programmes of staff development designed to build understanding and motivation around the changes being made, particularly around customer service and quality. This was problematic in criminal justice where, at the centre of proceedings, was a reluctant user of the service, namely the defendant or offender. Quality initiatives remained therefore at the margins, focused for example on the provision of improved facilities at police stations and courts, better signposting and information provision, and more customer service training (Raine and Willson, 1996).

The result was that, whereas in other services there were attempts to support staff in making difficult personal transitions in their practice, in criminal justice this was very limited. Consistent with its own ethos, the stick, rather than the carrot, was used. An example of this was the way in which the work patterns were increasingly standardised in services such as the police, the magistrates' courts and the probation service. In the interests of efficiency, transparency, performance and its measurement, clear specification was required of the conditions for intervention, methods to be used and the standards of outputs to be achieved. In part this was required by legislative process as, for example, in the tighter sentencing regimes imposed in the 1991 Criminal Justice Act and in the 1997 Crime (Sentences) Act. It was reinforced by policy documentation including Guidance, Circulars and Advice Notes and by the publication of recommendations from the criminal justice inspectorates. An example was the publication of national standards for practice within the probation service. This central process was replicated at local level with each service producing its own internal policy documentation and procedural and good practice guidelines.

The rigorous application of standards meant that a price was paid in respect of individual initiative and responsibility for action by professional practitioners, who were increasingly alienated from their organisations.

3.7 Evaluation and conclusion

The story of the public service managerialist reforms as they affected criminal justice is one of inconsistent and piecemeal direction on the part of ministers and reluctant participation on the part of most agencies. First, in the absence of an agreed purpose for the reform of criminal justice itself (see Chapter 2), the intermediate goals of cost efficiency and service effectiveness became pre-eminent. In the absence of an agreed strategy for change, intervention by government was influenced by size of budget, ease of pickings and ministerial preference. The effort put into resisting the reforms by agencies, perhaps with only the Crown Prosecution Service as the exception, hampered any real potential for imaginative and innovative change driven by services themselves.

Second, it is arguable that the reforms could never have worked in criminal justice in any case since the three prerequisites for their success were absent. There was no market and hence no real consumer in criminal justice, and no real prospect of creating one given the special character of the key 'customer' (the offender) and difficulties for providers around market entry and exit. Without even a quasi-market in place, there was no real basis for competition between providers (Le Grand, 1990).

Together, it is argued, these two factors resulted in managerialism; that is, the introduction of a variety of methods and techniques into practice without a meaningful context. They were management tools introduced without a broad understanding, a theory or a praxis of management, and without consent to or support for the change process within agencies.

Managerialism can be, and was, heavily criticised. Its characteristically extreme rationalism in decision-making was arguably inappropriate within a complex and pluralistic setting; its simplistic conversion of service users into consumers made no sense when the service user was an offender; the use of false competition created inequality and artificiality in the contracting process which, in turn, created a paper-chase of new administrative demands.

At the same time, wrapped up in the reforms were a number of important ideas and developments which had, and have, the potential to progress criminal justice, and which can be all too easily overlooked. Among these was the impetus to needs-driven rather than provider-driven services, propelled by a formulae basis for budget calculation. Important, too, was the demand for transparency and the provision of public information in services and service performance as part of a revised approach to public accountability. There was also an emphasis on service quality which, though not necessarily realised, was to persist. Of on-going significance was the focus on service efficiency and practice effectiveness, known within criminal justice as the 'what works' debate. Above all, the identification of purchasers (or commissioners) and providers of service, though never converted into structural reform in most criminal justice settings, facilitated the realisation that public services did not necessarily need to be publicly provided. This made explicit the potential for a mixed economy of provision (public, private and voluntary).

The immediate effect of the imposition of managerial reforms on a reluctant audience was, first, to drive a deep division between government and agencies normally characterised by their conservatism. Second was the deleterious effect on staff morale, particularly among professional groups. The longer term effect is more difficult to estimate. Certainly at the end of the 1990s, variations on managerialism were embedded in criminal justice, as in the wider public service sector, in the UK and abroad, suggesting a continuing influence. At the same time, Labour's commitment to end the introduction of markets into public services, if implemented, must affect the shape of future reform. Rather than dismantling what limited markets currently exist, a more successful way forward might be to concentrate on growing the mixed economy for which the market was itself simply a tool in a transition process from a paternalistic and bureaucratic model of social welfare to a model more appropriate for the future (James, 1997). Getting beyond the market means getting beyond means to ends in criminal justice. It means actively pump-priming private and voluntary sector initiatives to generate a mixed economy; identifying the needs of offenders in addition to the needs of service providers; and, above all, agreeing an overall purpose and change strategy in criminal justice such that strategy drives behaviour and not the other way around.

CHAPTER FOUR

The administrative processing of criminal justice

4.1 Introduction

The political ideology and managerialist agenda of the Thatcher administration in the 1980s was in contrast to what had gone before (see Chapter 3). But it is important also to recognise the other forces for change that have worked upon criminal justice, many over the full post-war period. In this chapter the focus is on a different and longer term dynamic which has also played a significant part in the shaping of criminal justice. This dynamic is identified here as 'administrative processing' and consists of three closely connected processes: complexification, bureaucratisation and professionalisation. The identification of this dynamic is important because in many ways it can be thought of as being in direct contrast to the dynamics previously discussed of politicisation and managerialism. Both of these were pursued in an agenda of simplification, de-bureaucratisation and de-professionalisation.

Chapter 2 described how the complex political agenda of social order was narrowed to a law and order issue, then to a crime and punishment agenda and subsequently to a preoccupation with sentencing. Chapter 3 described the process by which the managerialist agenda had the effect of devaluing the contribution of different professional groups working within criminal justice. Administrative processing, running alongside and threading through those dynamics, arguably begins to explain some of the unexpected outcomes and apparent contradictions of the political and managerial reforms of the 1980s and 1990s. At times the dynamic acted as a brake on reform – a sieve through which proposed changes had to pass – while at other times it confused or even confounded intended developments. What this dynamic also represents is a particular style and way of conducting criminal justice operational activity based on long experience of policy-making and policy implementation.

This chapter explores, with examples, the nature of each of the three processes (complexification, bureaucratisation and professionalisation) which make up the dynamic. It then proceeds to consider the impact of the dynamic as a whole upon the landscape of criminal justice. We begin by identifying the concept of administrative processing itself, highlighting its key features.

4.2 Key features of administrative processing

The dynamic focuses on *how* criminal justice works (Zedner, 1993). With much of the emphasis being on the operation of policies and practices, it is an important dynamic in giving substance and providing detail to the broad direction of change signalled by politicians and leaders, but with inevitably less attention paid to vision and strategic direction. This process, it is argued, has several key features that inform its implementation.

First is the predilection for *continuity* which is reflected, for example, in a general respect by practitioners for tradition and for the conventional ways of doing things. That is not to say that change is necessarily resisted; on the contrary, the administrative processing of criminal justice is a story of change and development. Proposed modifications, however, are more likely to be incremental and evolutionary, building on and evaluated against the practices and standards in currency, rather than radically dismantling and rebuilding. If discontinuity is to be tolerated, it is because it is perceived within a broader framework of continuing development. This trait may find expression in the form of resistance by practitioners to the introduction of change by others, particularly if the change is not perceived to be in step and sequence with the strand of development that they had envisaged. Sometimes the political force for change is such that practitioner resistance is overwhelmed. But perhaps concessions have to be made and practitioners achieve success in delaying implementation until further research is completed or in making adjustments to the policy. Such adjustments have the effect of 'rounding off the rougher edges', in the way classically attributed to the working of the senior civil service in relation to policy-making.

Second is the *fragmentation* which characterises both the structure and implementation of criminal justice agencies and their practice, such that the tendency in policy-making has been to focus on quite specific aspects, for example, of policing or judicial administration, and to make changes with insufficient regard to the whole picture. The result has been that criminal justice as a policy area has developed by a process of accretion of new procedures and in a largely incremental fashion. Moreover, because a number of different agencies are involved in the process, some organised and managed at national level, others distinctly local in structure and culture, and because various different professional and non-professional groups are involved, there have been obvious inconsistencies and even contradictions of intent as well as of practice. Inevitably this increasing complexity has inhibited the implementation of radical change.

Third is the *practitioner focus* together with its underpinning ideologies, mores and codes of conduct. Though these are not consistent among themselves, they do generally represent and reflect the outcomes of a well-intentioned, if relatively closed, practitioner community and are to be distinguished from the official position and perspective of their particular agencies (Rutherford, 1993). Rutherford identified three distinct clusters of values and beliefs which shaped the daily work and professional careers of criminal justice practitioners. The first of these (described as the punishment credo) embraced the punitive degradation of offenders. The second (described as the efficiency credo) was less moralistic and more concerned with management practices of pragmatism, efficiency and expediency. The third (described as the caring credo) centred upon a cluster of libertarian and humanitarian values towards suspects, accused persons and prisoners, as well as to victims and others caught up in the criminal justice process.

Rutherford commented upon the complexity of the interplay of these three different credos, and encountered several instances where the actual working practices and culture were out of tune with the official position and perspective of the particular agency. He pointed, for example, to

> ... the chasm that exists between the agency's mission statements, which often parade values and sentiments that go to the core of Credo Three, and routine practice. This institutionalised disson-

ance between words and deeds leaves the Credo Three practitioner in tune with formal purposes but out of step with working traditions and culture. (Rutherford, 1993, p. 160)

Such credos themselves act as powerful forces in shaping or blocking new initiatives to ensure alignment with the prevailing views of professionals and practitioners. Important here, too, is the paternalistic tendency of much practitioner professionalism; the well-intentioned thinking that underlies most of what is proposed and implemented in the name of reform but which may also be viewed as self-serving.

Fourth, and arising out of the fragmentation of criminal justice between different agencies and the diversity of professional practitioner groupings, is the requirement for *co-operative working* between the individual practitioners and agencies which share this professionalised and institutionalised world. This is reflected in the number of inter-agency working arrangements that link staff from different organisations at all levels. Differences of philosophy and policy priorities there may be, but these are usually confined and carefully managed to avoid conflict, because the end requirement is to deliver work together or at least in parallel. At the same time the network of co-operation tends to be narrowly and exclusively drawn around the larger public sector organisations. This means that other significant contributors to the process may be excluded from the debate and from some decision-making around the operation of 'the system' – for example, organisations in the voluntary sector. This organisational exclusivity has also tended to ring-fence criminal justice and minimise its connections with other social policy issues, such as poverty, health and education.

Fifth is the concern with the development and elaboration of *procedure* in the form of principles, standards and protocols for implementation. The legacies of managerialism have included more streamlined and simplified procedures and a greater propensity to 'cut corners' in order to save money or time. In contrast, those of the dynamic of administrative processing have been lengthening, increasing sophistication and elaboration of procedures. In many respects this reflects the concerns of practitioners and professionals to protect and enhance principles of justice and due process. An example is the introduction of procedures requiring the disclosure in advance of the prosecution case to the defence and, more recently, of the defence case to the prosecution to avoid 'ambushes' by one side or the other in court during trials. At times it has reflected a measure of self-interest on the part of practitioners and their organisations in 'buying' time and buffering themselves against unwelcome pressures. The increase in delays in the completion of cases through the courts is probably the most obvious illustration of the dynamic of administrative processing at work during the period under review (Home Office, 1997).

Finally, and perhaps for similar reasons, the dynamic tends to be *long term* in its horizons. New procedures and practices are preferably the outcomes of careful consideration, rigorous piloting and research. The effect is to minimise the risk of oversight and unanticipated outcomes. But a price may be paid, not just in terms of higher costs and tardier progress but also in generating solutions to problems that are already out-of-date and ineffective by the time the solutions are implemented.

In conclusion, these various traits may be understood collectively in three distinct processes that have characterised the dynamic of administrative processing in criminal justice. First is a *complexification* process by which we refer to the accretive tendency in the development of policy and procedures. Second is a *bureaucratisation* process with a focus on organisational and institutional development. Third is a *professionalisation* process, in which the exercise of duty and responsibility in criminal justice is increasingly dominated by those with qualifications considered appropriate for practice.

4.3 The complexification of criminal justice

In many respects the story of evolving and ever-more complex procedures in criminal justice mirrors experience in other arenas of public policy. The steady accretion of new procedures, each devised to resolve a particular problem or oversight that has become apparent with experience of the preceding initiative, is characteristic of much policy-making. Arguably, this process is amplified in criminal justice, first because of its basis in incrementally established caselaw and a legalistic framework and, second, because of the way in which legislation is constructed and passed through two Houses of Parliament in the UK. Pressure of parliamentary time, together with protracted and uncertain committee stages through which draft legislation must pass, make it easier to amend, rather than to create wholly new laws. The result has been to reinforce a 'ratcheting' effect in the formative process of creating primary and secondary legislation. The considerable time involved in the parliamentary process has encouraged the development of non-legislative policy tools such that, in the period under review, there has been a marked increase in the use and sophistication of government circulars, guidance, letters, advice and other instruments of official policy development. Such processes and tools have been replicated at local level within agencies of criminal justice, creating an appearance of order and increasing regularity, but often with the effect of augmenting the scope for ambiguity of interpretation and expectation. This, in turn, has tended to generate another round of processes designed to address loopholes, possible malpractice, abuse or negligence.

The effect of complexification is not simply to delay implementation, though that is important, but more significantly, to obfuscate the more obvious connection between the cause and effect of any intervention. This has the potential to generate a 'domino effect' where a slight slip can trigger an unexpectedly large response. Levers for change are therefore difficult to identify and the outcomes of interventions difficult to predict as complexity theory is a close relation of catastrophe theory and chaos theory, both of which try to explain how and why highly ordered systems can self-destruct.

The process of complexification and its implications for criminal justice are illuminated by reference to two case studies drawn from the police and the courts. In the case of the police, the example presented is that of police procedures for interviewing suspects, which were the subject of extensive overhaul in the 1980s under the Police and Criminal Evidence Act 1984 (Home Office, 1984), and again in 1997. The example illustrates how the introduction of more procedures added complexity to existing processes and uncovered further potential for abuse, inviting successive rounds of proceduralisation. The second example, from the magistrates' courts, concerns the introduction of new pre-trial practice rules in the mid 1980s that were further extended in the mid-1990s, and illustrates the impact of proceduralisation on delays in hearing cases.

PACE legislation: a case study of complexification

The background to the Police and Criminal Evidence Act 1984 (PACE) was the Royal Commission on Criminal Procedure, which reported in 1981 (Home Office, 1981). This was initiated by concerns about policing methods in investigating cases and the ways in which evidence might be gathered and confessions elicited from suspects. The report advocated a set of prescribed systems and procedures to be followed to prevent police malpractice and give greater public confidence in the process. Following the recommendations, formal custody records were introduced logging all the actions taken during the detention of suspects. The right to legal advice free of charge was endorsed through the establishment of duty solicitor schemes, whereby solicitors would either be at police stations or be available to attend there at immediate notice (Ashworth, 1994).

The main procedural changes were enacted through the Police and Criminal Evidence Act 1984 (Home Office, 1984). This piece of legislation laid down in statute the new rules and procedural-requirements governing (1) the way suspects were questioned by investigating officers and (2) the rights of suspects. It was a significant step in terms of the development of a framework and regime within which the police would have to conduct themselves. It set out, for example, the duties and responsibilities of the custody officer who, independent of the investigation, would be responsible for ensuring compliance with the rules and the welfare of those in custody. This included authorising their release for interview, informing suspects of their rights of access to legal advice and documenting on custody records all the actions and decisions taken in relation to each person detained in custody. The custody record was to be the guard against 'informal, off-the-record, chats'. In addition, PACE introduced the contemporaneous audio-recording of all interviews.

With the enactment of PACE, the police would have to work in a more disciplined manner if they were to work within the bounds defined in law. This would address public concerns about police malpractice, which had been amplified by some of the notorious miscarriages of justice that had come to light in the period. However, subsequent research findings failed to confirm the assertion that malpractice could no longer occur. McConville et al. (1991) found that many custody officers were not adhering strictly to the

PACE regulations and appeared on occasions to be ignoring breaches of the associated Code of Practice. The research high-lighted instances of collusion by custody officers in such infringe-ments, or coercion to overlook malpractice by more assertive detectives. 'Off-the-record' interviews were still taking place and custody records were not necessarily to be relied upon as a com-prehensive account of the actions taken. Reiner (1992, p. 1) con-cluded that 'the idea of the custody officer as an independent check ... has proved chimerical'. Revisions were subsequently made to the PACE Code of Practice in 1991 with further proposals made for the videoing (rather than audio-taping) of interviews with suspects.

The pre-trial process: a case study of complexification

The second example concerns rules for disclosure of information about each case to the other party in advance of trials in the magistrates' court. Like the regulations governing police practices, the matter of pre-trial procedures was successively reviewed in the 1980s and 1990s. In 1985 (under the Magistrates' Courts (Advance Information) Rules), new regulations were introduced requiring the prosecution to disclose to the defence the details of its case and the evidence to be presented in advance of the court deciding the mode of trial (Home Office, 1985). These 'advance disclosure' rules were designed to apply particularly to 'triable either way' cases, although in practice the Crown Prosecution Ser-vice tended to apply them to 'summary' cases as well.

The disclosure rules were devised to ensure that defendants could make an informed decision not only about the mode of trial but also about how to plead. They meant that, on request, the prosecution would provide the accused with a summary of the written statements and documents upon which they were proposing to rely. The exceptions here were where there was a risk of inti-midation of witnesses or of interference with the course of justice.

The introduction of disclosure rules exemplifies the complexifi-cation process in two ways. First, it amounted to an additional duty or step in the process that was designed to add fairness into the court process, reflecting a belief that the defence had a right to know the evidence that would be presented by the prosecution. Second, it meant that more time would be needed to perform that task. The introduction of disclosure significantly extended the length of time between first court appearance and final disposition because the professionals (the CPS and the defence advocates) were unable, or reluctant, to operate the new requirement within the traditional timeframes. As a result, during the 1980s, the courts became increasingly overloaded with incomplete cases. Requests for adjournments became the norm in all but the most minor of cases. For example, the defence might ask for a two-week adjournment, claiming at the hearing that the disclosure information had only just been received from the CPS, or was still awaited. The CPS, in turn, might ask to adjourn for a fortnight, pleading that the details of the case had only recently arrived from the police and, therefore, more time was needed to review the case and to issue advance disclosure.

The frustration of magistrates at the slow pace of case progressions prompted further research into the causes of delays in the courts and a working group was established by the Home Office in 1989 (the Pre-Trial Issues Group) to devise a timetable and standard procedure for the pre-trial process. Among the outcomes of this group was a recommendation for a standard five/six-week period between charge and first hearing. This was proposed by the CPS to allow the police time to prepare files and give the CPS lawyers time to review them ahead of providing disclosure to the defence. This timetable was implemented and helped in areas where case progressions had been especially slow. Elsewhere, where case progression had been faster, it resulted in a deterioration in time-scales because the new timetable became the standard to which police and CPS worked. This illustrates a disbenefit of standardisation and an unintended consequence of complexification.

4.4 The bureaucratisation of criminal justice

A second strand of the dynamic of administrative processing is 'bureaucratisation'. This refers to administrative processing as it affects organisational development. It refers specifically to the three characteristics originally developed by Max Weber and applied elsewhere to public service reform in the 1980s Thatcher reforms (James, 1994). The three characteristics are hierarchy of structure; division of labour; and assertion of power through authority related to role, position and function rather than coercion.

These characteristics were reproduced in criminal justice settings in two distinctive ways during the 1980s and 1990s. The first was the growing fragmentation and reconstruction of the existing organisational framework, achieved partly by privatisation and partly by the deliberate separation of responsibilities for policy-making and for provision. The second was the introduction of new agencies either to fill gaps and provide new functions or to clarify existing functions and take them over – a process which we describe as 'agencyfication'. Both the organisational fragmentation/reconstruction and agencyfication processes incorporated task subdivision (division of labour), hierarchical restructuring and revised patterns authority.

Examples of the separation of policy-making and provision were the 'Next Steps' agencies created following the Ibbs Report (Cabinet Office, 1989). In criminal justice the Prison Services Agency and the Court Service Agency were created, each with its own structure and chief executive. As an example of privatisation, while not extensively introduced in criminal justice, the building and running of new prisons was contracted out (Chapter 3).

In the absence of perceived rapid progress, the mechanism of competition was increasingly employed in the late 1980s and 1990s (James, 1994). This had manifested itself in the health service in the creation of a quasi-market of purchasers and providers, with health authorities and 'fund-holding' GPs buying treatment for their patients from health providers. In local government it took the form of compulsory competitive tendering regimes, initially focused on 'blue collar' direct labour forces, but later planned for some professional services such as architecture, IT, finance and personnel. In central government it was expressed in the market testing policy of the early 1990s, while in the public utilities and certain other public service contexts, it took the form of privatisation (James, 1994).

Agencyfication

The second characteristic of the bureaucratisation process in criminal justice was the addition of new agencies either to fill gaps and undertake new functions or to clarify existing ones and take them over. While the creation of the Prison Service Agency and the Court Service Agency represented major structural change within criminal justice, the tasks to be undertaken had long been established. The creation of new responsibilities, or new constructions of existing responsibilities, represented a further force for change. An example was the creation of the Criminal Cases Review Commission in response to a recommendation by the Royal Commission on Criminal Justice (Runciman, 1993). This new independent organisation was set up to review cases of alleged miscarriages of justice, an activity previously undertaken within the Home Office. Another example was the creation of the Magistrates' Courts Inspectorate in 1992 to undertake routine inspections of each local area service and to provide leadership on 'good practice' through the conduct of thematic studies (HM Magistrates' Courts Service Inspectorate, 1996).

Particularly significant for the future of criminal justice were the creation of the Crown Prosecution Service and Victim Support. Both were to have a profound effect on the process and priorities of criminal justice in England and Wales.

The Crown Prosecution Service: a case study in bureaucratisation

The establishment of the Crown Prosecution Service in 1986 marked a major change in the statutory framework as well as in the operational arrangements for criminal justice in England and Wales. It marked the end of police responsibility for both deciding whether or not to prosecute and for undertaking the prosecution of offences in court. The new body was set up as a national organisation under the Prosecution of Offences Act 1985 (which was closely linked with the PACE legislation). Prior to this Act the police and the Director of Public Prosecutions had been responsible for criminal prosecutions. Many criticisms had been levelled at this arrangement but chief among them was the concern that the police were acting both as investigator and prosecutor and that the crime control function of investigation could be in conflict with the interests of justice and due process, particularly where prosecutions were pursued without sufficient evidence. From a Royal Commission set up in 1978 came the key recommendation that an independent agency should be established in the interests of civil liberties to review and conduct the prosecution of criminal cases and to encourage consistency in prosecution policy and practice (Home Office, 1981).

Upon establishment, a Code of Conduct was drawn up for

Crown Prosecutors which set out the new organisation's review and decision-making role and documented its values and principles as independence, objectivity and fairness. The Code established two important tests for prosecution policy: 'evidential sufficiency' and 'public interest' (Davies et al., 1995).

As well as its impact through standardising and specifying prosecution policy, the CPS has had a profound effect upon the whole process of criminal justice. As a national organisation it was immediately able to assert itself in relations with locally organised agencies (the police, magistrates' courts and probation). For example, the time-scales developed for the pre-trial process by the Pre-Trial Issues Group were strongly influenced by the arguments of the CPS. However, it was criticised for putting its own resourcing problems ahead of key justice concerns in exercising its power of discontinuance and delaying the processing of cases.

Victim Support: a case study of bureaucratisation

The case of Victim Support was especially interesting for two reasons: first, it represented the institutionalisation of a new activity, the provision of advisory and emotional support to victims of crime; second, it was a non-statutory service whose services were principally undertaken by unpaid volunteers.

The initial impetus of the 'victim movement' in England and Wales drew on similar initiatives in the USA and Canada. Mainly through the pioneering work of a small number of locally organised victim support schemes, the idea developed rapidly in the UK and had an increasing effect on thinking and practice in criminal justice. By the mid-1980s local schemes had been established in most towns. They typically comprised a co-ordinator who would contact the police each day and be provided with details of new victims of crime, and a group of volunteers who would visit or telephone each victim to offer emotional and practical support.

Formation of the National Association of Victim Support Schemes – an 'umbrella' organisation for local victim support schemes with a London base – was an important step in creating the ethos of a unitary organisation and one close to government (Rock, 1990). Partly through skilful leadership and partly because the message struck a chord with public servants and politicians alike, the Home Office became a strong supporter of the movement and provided an increasing proportion of funding. Policy initiatives from the Home Office during the 1990s increasingly reflected the growing influence of the Association. These included the proposal to consult victims on the early release of prisoners and the drafting of a Victim's Charter (Home Office, 1996a).

The impact of Victim Support on criminal justice was all the more remarkable given its non-statutory position, voluntary sector status and volunteer dependency. This newcomer organisation was able to effect change in police attitudes and practice, inspire the CPS to review its practices in this context, persuade the courts to surrender space and resources to accommodate victim support work, and the probation service to take on new responsibilities in relation to victims as well as offenders.

4.5 The professionalisation of criminal justice

The third strand of the dynamic of administrative processing in criminal justice is 'professionalisation'. This is in distinct contrast with the de-professionalisation process generated by the political and managerialist reforms of the period, and yet has run in parallel with them. By professionalisation we refer to a process by which the pre-eminence of expertise in a particular occupational area has the potential to assume a monopoly of provision. This is based on the three criteria of approved qualification, commitment to agreed mores and codes of practice, and capacity to attract the confidence of a lay clientele (James, 1994; Freidson, 1970).

As with complexification and bureaucratisation, it is possible to identify a number of aspects within the professionalisation process as it developed in the 1980s and 1990s. Particularly significant for the dynamic of administrative processing in criminal justice has been, first, the steady but significant extension of the paid professional into areas traditionally occupied by the laity, and, second, the standardisation of professional practice. The first is illustrated by a case study on the lay magistracy; the second by the development of charging standards in the CPS.

The lay magistracy: a case study of professionalisation

Criticisms of the lay magistracy have been long-standing, with concerns about the recruitment process, the social composition of the bench and inconsistency and undue leniency in sentencing. The

Magistrates' Association had worked hard to address these concerns throughout the 1980s and 1990s by publishing more information about the magistracy, supporting more openness and encouraging more applications from local people to join the lay bench, issuing national sentencing guidelines to local courts and promoting more training. These developments met with a mixed response from magistrates themselves, some of whom were concerned that their discretion was being narrowed by the sentencing guidelines and their lay status undermined by the amount of training now expected of them.

In practice the issue was broader. The role of lay magistrates was being squeezed by professionals from three directions: from stipendiary magistrates, from justices' clerks and from the police. The succession of additional stipendiary magistrate appointments made from the late 1980s onwards was widely perceived in the magistracy as a threat to the lay system. Repeated statements of commitment to lay justice from the Lord Chancellor failed to provide reassurance. At a more mundane level, a recurrent complaint of lay magistrates was that stipendiaries were 'creaming off' the more complex, often more interesting, cases including remand hearings and the longer trials.

Others felt that their justices' clerks (their legal advisers and chief administrators) were predisposed towards stipendiary magistrates, which was often the case. As professional lawyers themselves, and with considerable experience of the disadvantages of a lay system, many justices' clerks had long favoured a stipendiary system for its greater consistency, toughness on offenders and speedier pace of work. Indeed, many had seen the benefits of stipendiaries first-hand when they had 'borrowed' them from other areas to hear particular extended and complex cases, perceived to be problematical for a lay bench. This had led them to think that a permanent appointment in their patch would be an effective way of reducing delays, achieving more consistency and challenging the idiosyncrasies of the lay bench. A number of justices' clerks also acted as part-time stipendiaries, and relished the opportunity to join the judiciary on a full-time basis.

Alongside all this, the justices' clerks themselves provided a second pressure on the lay magistracy through their pursuit of delegated powers to act in place of appointed justices. The Justices' Clerks' Society continually argued for such powers, although often the efforts were thwarted by the influence at national level of the

Magistrates' Association which, usually, was strongly opposed to the idea. However, accompanying the establishment of a new Family Court system in 1990 were new procedural requirements that involved the delegation of substantial new powers to justices' clerks. With concerns growing about the tardiness of court processing, there were further pressures from justices' clerks to be given powers to act as single justices in hearings. An initiative at Bexley magistrates' court illustrates this. Here defendants were required to appear before the clerk (not magistrates) for a pre-hearing at which matters such as legal aid, representation and hearing dates would be dealt with. Although the scheme had a questionable basis in law, it was quickly adopted by justices' clerks at other courts and, indeed, attracted support from the Home Office because it increased case completion rates (Raine, 1994). The Magistrates' Association registered strong opposition to the scheme because it was felt to infringe their authority and reduce what they regarded as 'judicial' decisions to the status of 'administrative processing'.

The third instance of the squeezing of the lay magistracy by professionals came from the police. A recent example here was the extension to police officers of powers to attach conditions to bail previously reserved for the judiciary. This was made possible under the Criminal Justice and Public Order Act 1994 following a recommendation in the report of the Royal Commission on Criminal Justice (Runciman, 1993). Prior to this, the police had two options after charging suspects: they could release them on police bail (which was unconditional) to attend court at a later date, or they could hold them overnight in police cells to appear before magistrates on the following morning. There the prosecution would typically argue either that the defendant should be remanded in custody until the date of trial or, if the court was inclined to grant bail, that certain conditions should be attached, such as a curfew or weekly reporting at a local police station.

The key arguments cited in favour of extending the power to the police to attach conditions to bail mainly concerned more efficient processing of defendants – namely, through a significant reduction in the number of people kept overnight in police cells, a reduction in the number of 'overnight remand' cases for magistrates' courts to have to deal with and a corresponding reduction in the court-based work of the Crown Prosecution Service and defence solicitors. This meant that the responsibility for constraining a person's liberty (through conditions such as curfew or reporting) was passed from an independent judiciary to the executive. It also meant that this would often be done without the benefit of representations by the defence. It was an act of professionalising bail with conditions, by extending the responsibility for imposition from a part-time volunteer magistracy to full-time trained custody officers within the police. If the professionalisation process was intended to produce better decision-making, research findings suggested that it failed to do so. A study based on six local areas highlighted inconsistency and idiosyncrasy in the application of bail conditions by the police and found little evidence of special training having been given to custody officers to equip them for this new role (Raine and Willson, 1997).

The CPS and charging standards: a case study of professionalisation

Standardising professional practices was the other aspect of professionalisation of relevance to the dynamic of administrative processing in criminal justice. An example was the development by the CPS of 'charging standards' for the police and their own lawyers to use. This is relevant because, in creating the CPS, the decision was taken to employ only qualified lawyers to review cases and decide on prosecution. Thus the CPS was established as a highly professionalised organisation. Charging standards were designed and agreed with the police initially for three categories of offence, these being 'driving offences', 'public order offences' and 'offences against the person'. The intention was to extend the approach across all the main categories of criminal offence. The category of 'offences against the person' had often been contentious due to differences in prosecuting practices regarding 'grievous bodily harm' and the lesser charge of 'actual bodily harm'.

The rationale for the standards, then, was equity and consistency in prosecution policy. This extended beyond the simple definition of the offence to taking into account any associated circumstances (for example, degree of harm caused). This had unanticipated consequences such that following their introduction, the numbers of assault cases being dealt with in magistrates' courts increased significantly while numbers at the Crown Court declined by a similar proportion. While in 1989, only about 3,700 people were convicted of the (new) offence of common assault (as defined in s. 39 of the Criminal Justice Act 1988), by 1996, that figure had risen to over 25,000. In contrast, a corresponding drop occurred in the numbers charged with the more serious offence of actual bodily harm (as defined in s. 47 of the Offences Against the Person Act 1861). The standards may have ensured greater consistency in prosecution practices, but compared with the previous position, they had also brought about a down-grading of offences enabling more to be dealt with as summary justice in the lower courts. Consequently, more victims were dissatisfied with the way criminal justice worked, perceiving offenders to have 'got away' with unduly lenient charges and to have obtained lesser sentences as a result (Davies et al., 1995).

4.6 Conclusions

This chapter has focused on the dynamic of administrative processing in criminal justice. The key features were identified as continuity, fragmentation, a practitioner focus, co-operative working, the development and elaboration of procedure and a long-term view. The dynamic finds expression through the three processes of complexification, bureaucratisation and professionalisation, and several examples and case studies of these have been presented. What, then, has been the significance of the dynamic for the development of criminal justice in the period under review?

Arguably there were three main outcomes. First, the process gave momentum to the growing tendency to regard criminal justice agencies as members of a 'criminal justice system'. Much of the activity was about identifying and filling gaps of function or process. The individuality of agency behaviour, previously perceived as appropriate to agency function and professional competence, became perceived as undesirable. The result was to boost inter-agency activity. Joint planning was encouraged, for example, through the creation of Area Committees of the Consultative Council on Criminal Justice, established on the recommendation of Lord Woolf's report on the Strangeways prison riots (Woolf, 1991) At operational levels, joint working was encouraged, for example, through court user groups which brought together representatives of all the agencies working at each local court.

This momentum was subsequently picked up by the New Labour administration which again emphasised the notion of a criminal justice 'system' and the need for efficiency in processing between agencies, with the hint of stronger regional networking and possible co-terminosity with police areas. It also represented a challenge to the notion of an 'independent judiciary' and contributed to down-grading the status and authority of the court. This was evidenced, for example, in the comparative ease with which the new and professionalised CPS was able to influence case progression time-scales at magistrates' courts.

Second, the dynamic acted as a foil, in effect a block, to those processes germane to the political and managerialist reforms of the Conservative administration between 1979 and 1997, namely the processes of simplification, of de-bureaucratisation and of de-professionalisation (see Chapters 2 and 3). The effect was to create an extraordinary level of conflict within criminal justice. Most explicit was the conflict between the Home Secretary and those managers who were perceived to be progressing the reforms, and the professionals who were perceived to be standing their ground or blocking change. It was for this level of conflict and for the ways in which he was perceived to exacerbate it, that Home Secretary, Michael Howard, became particularly renowned.

Third, because the dynamic worked at operational and practice levels, it acted as a sieve through which all new policy would have to pass to achieve implementation. The effect, at best, was to distance practitioners from the policy-making process. Sometimes it resulted in activity at different levels going in different directions at the same time. At worst, with the assertive political leadership of the period and the managerialist impatience for change to be confronted, it was inevitable that conflicts would arise between the world of practice and the leadership at the Home Office and Lord Chancellor's Department. This disturbed the calmer, mutually supportive relationship of past years between the paid officials and the elected representatives.

The immediate effect was of 'stop–go', which frustrated radical change and also ensured that reform would often be piecemeal and therefore potentially ineffective, if not counterproductive. The result was to leave the incoming Labour Government with a heritage of disorder. Also important was loss of morale among professionals in conflict with political and managerial change, and the associated breakdown in trust – always very fragile – between policy-makers and those responsible for its implementation.

CHAPTER FIVE

Criminal justice, public voice and participation

5.1 Introduction

The argument of this chapter is that public voice and participation has formed a key dimension in the construction and articulation of change in criminal justice policy and practice through the 1980s and 1990s. The phrase 'public voice and participation' is used to refer to what the public, sometimes as users of criminal justice services, expect, say and do and also to the ways in which these messages and actions are heard by the state and its institutions. Public voice and participation is the fourth key dynamic in the shaping of criminal justice in the period under review.

Public voice and participation relies on a dynamic process whereby perceptions and expectations about crime and criminal justice are transmitted between the public and representatives of the state, and vice versa. The extent to which the messages received in either direction are consistent with those transmitted is questionable – in other words, the extent to which the state understands the public mood in relation to crime and criminal justice and, in turn, the extent to which the public understands the realities surrounding the state's response. As with other communication systems, much depends on processes in operation, and it is necessary to recognise the potential for misunderstanding, distortion, misinterpretation and misinformation in both directions. The argument is that some of the main problems for criminal justice policy and practice during the period under review reflected the fact that public opinion was not always sufficiently understood or taken into account by the politicians and policy-makers and, conversely, that the public were generally not well informed either about the circumstances surrounding the problem of crime or about the criminal justice agencies and their responses.

The chapter begins by identifying the complex nature of public voice itself, clarifying the language in use and different conceptual positions represented by that language. It proceeds to explore the development of public voice in relation to criminal justice over the 1980s and 1990s. The argument is that the development has not been strictly populist – though it is easily perceived as such – and that populism provides a simplistic framework for viewing a more complex change phenomenon. The chapter goes on to trace a shift in the period away from the expression of public voice based on citizenship and representation to one based on consumerism and potentially on human rights, and to consider the consequences of this shift.

5.2 The nature of public voice

The term 'public voice' can have different meanings for different people. It is used here as a generic term to accommodate a range of positions about the basis for public participation in issues of state and public policy. Some positions are more developed than others, some clearly identifiable with core ideologies, others incompletely borrowed from other contexts, countries and sectors. Each position has its own language, though in practice these languages have been mixed up and are often used ambiguously. Most of all, the social realities which these languages represent are dynamic in the period under review.

Within the concept of 'public voice' it is possible to identify at least six contemporary threads: the first identifies public voice with public representation; the second relates it to citizenship and the third to rights; the fourth relies on empowerment; the fifth relies on public accountability as the logic for involvement; and the sixth is based on the public as consumers of public services.

The argument in this chapter is that there has been a shift in the nature of public voice and participation during the period under review from one based on representation and citizenship to one based on consumerism and potentially on human rights. This shift has had consequences both for the ways in which public voice gets heard and (in conjunction with the other key dimensions discussed in Chapters 2, 3 and 4) has had implications for the ways in which criminal justice policy and practice have developed over the period. In order to make this argument, it is necessary to explain the six positions in more detail.

Representation

The first and most acknowledged way in which public voice gets presented and heard is through the public body or the elected representative (that is, through the MP or local councillor). For elected members there is a persistent tension between representing the electorate, representing government and representing themselves. The classic example of this from criminal justice is over the death penalty where the views of the public, as indicated by polls, have consistently differed from those of the public representatives. Normally this tension is side-stepped by elected representatives claiming to act 'in the public interest', with little or no supporting evidence.

Where the equilibrium in that tension is not maintained, where the elected member is not perceived to act in the public interest, where that public interest is deeply divided, or where the representative is perceived to act partially or for personal gain, the model of representation falls down as its credibility is dependent upon an ethic of altruism and truth (i.e. not cheating). It assumes some collectivity and some consensus on whose behalf representation can be made. Failure to maintain that equilibrium may result in others claiming to represent the public interest, in the pressing of partisan opinions and in loss of credibility for the elected representative. Examples of this in the period under review have involved both the police and the judiciary. A spate of revelations of serious miscarriages of justice, which hinged largely on the fabrication or withholding of vital evidence, did considerable damage to public confidence in the integrity of the police to represent the public interest. The judiciary, too, came in for critical scrutiny during the 1980s, and its reputation for fairness and impartiality was brought into question by a series of misplaced comments by judges in the courtroom, for example, in relation to the mode of dress of rape victims and the cultural habits of defendants from ethnic minority backgrounds (Ashworth and Hough, 1996).

Citizenship

If the notion of public voice through representation is based on the assumption of representative democracy, the notion of public voice based on citizenship is founded on an assumption of participative democracy. To be a citizen is to be entitled to participate in benefits which accrue from being a member of the state (of the 'city' in ancient times). These benefits normally include both political representation and participation but also access to social entitlements (such as protection, economic security, health and education). The concept therefore assumes a collectivity to which individuals belong and a set of responsibilities which accrue from so belonging.

The idea of public participation as the basis of citizenship has recently been highlighted in criminal justice by Faulkner and colleagues (Faulkner, 1996) for whom citizenship is closely tied to the regeneration of communities through self-help initiatives. This perspective on regeneration is to be distinguished from the 1970s' model of community development which was largely driven by professionals and involved the importing from outside of solutions to local problems.

There are difficulties with using citizenship as the basis for participation in criminal justice policy, not least because a key characteristic of the reluctant users of criminal justice (offenders) is their exclusion from community participation. This exclusion is reinforced by legislation in some instances, for example, the barring from appointment as a magistrate of those with a criminal record, or the non-applicability within a prison setting of those entitlements otherwise given to mentally ill people under the Mental Health Act 1983 (James, 1996).

Rights

Close to the concept of citizenship is the concept of civil rights. Civil rights are to be distinguished from human rights. Civil rights are a function of belonging to a 'civicus' (a city or state). Human rights are a function of belonging to humanity. In practice, human rights tend to be global, while civil rights tend to be national. While notions of civil rights and civil liberties have found their way into popular vocabulary, they are not a distinctive feature of British socio-legal heritage, certainly when compared with mainland Europe. Where the concept of rights appears in British law it usually relates to property, not civil rights. Unlike the concepts of representation or citizenship, its authority derives from individual privilege such as ownership. As a columnist on the *New York Times* commented:

Britain's curious lack of concern for civil liberties has several roots. Because its Parliamentary democracy evolved early, it has never developed a constitution or Bill of Rights. This deprived Britain of a culture of rights and the mechanisms to challenge abusive laws. The British have also enjoyed relatively benign rule. In recent decades, though, IRA terrorism has provided justification for draconian security laws. . . . The wide latitude enjoyed by the police is typical of the process that British Government holds over its citizens; powers that people in other democracies find distasteful.

(*New York Times*, 5 July 1997)

The concept of rights has made a recent appearance in public policy in the writings of Anna Coote and colleagues (Coote, 1997). Coote talks about rights in conjunction with responsibilities, thereby conferring a revised meaning whereby individual rights carry with them responsibilities to others. She distinguishes between substantive and procedural rights. Substantive rights may include social rights and responsibilities which are legally enforceable or generally agreed (for example, the right to be presumed innocent until proven guilty). An example of procedural rights are to be found in the Police and Criminal Evidence Act 1984 (PACE) regulations on the manner in which police interview suspects (Chapter 4). Substantive and procedural rights have often been confused in the period under review. For example, public charters such as the Victim's Charter or Patient's Charter were presented as though they were offering substantive rights, whereas in reality they conferred only procedural rights such as the right to assessment, to service, or to register a complaint.

Empowerment

While the language of empowerment presents as radical it is reserved in practice for the disempowered. It is used not of voters nor of citizens but of users of services. It depends on a paternalistic framework, where power is assumed to be given by some and received by others. Perhaps not surprisingly then, it is the language and framework widely adopted in public service where the assumption has been of state benevolence and service recipience, and of helping professions which assume the superiority born of expertise.

The contradiction between the language of empowerment and the ethical framework of paternalism which underpins it can be misleading. For example, the debate in recent years about patient empowerment in the Health Service has been less about the patient's right to treatment and more about the clinician's capacity to withhold it. Similarly, in criminal justice, the debate about prisoners' rights to a determined length of sentence has not been about prisoners' rights but instead about the Home Secretary's power to decide when release should take place.

Public accountability

While there has always been a tradition of accountability to the public within criminal justice, this developed in different forms in the period under review. Where the public gallery in courthouses and in Parliament once provided almost the only opportunity for openness and interface with citizens, developments in communications have generated new mechanisms, for example, in the form of open meetings and annual reports. As in other public services, not all such mechanisms have improved substantive accountability to the public. Indeed, it is argued that the development across the public sector of contracts of accountability between purchasers (commissioners) and providers of service has given an impression of transparency, robustness and reliability in accounting to the public which is not necessarily justified. Furthermore, demands for organisations and their staff to be seen to be accountable (through public efficiency targets and through performance measurement processes) have not always been accompanied by equivalent processes at government level (Nolan, 1997). But, as James (1994) has argued, there has been a general shift away from mechanisms for accountability located in a professional paradigm (qualification, membership of a professional body, maintenance of a client relationship) to those identified with a managerial one (accountability for budget, for staffing, for policies and for procedures).

Consumerism

The notion of the public as consumers or users of service is based on the ideology of the market as opposed to public service. The general critique of public service consumerism has been amply presented elsewhere (e.g. Potter, 1988; Pollitt, 1990; Pfeffer and Coote, 1991; Stewart and Walsh, 1992). Concern is limited here to consideration of the relevance and scope for application of such ideas to an area of the public sector in which 'consumer choice' might appear minimal and where much of the core service is provided under conditions of state coercion. Here much of the vocabulary, such as 'customer-orientation', 'consumer sovereignty', has limited relevance (Barron and Scott, 1992; Jones, 1993; Lacey, 1994; Easton and Rawlings, 1995).

In criminal courts, for instance, the customer is not easily defined. While defendants appear centre-stage and are the subject of the verdict and sentencing decisions of the court, the notion of defendants as 'consumers' is not straightforward and limited in relation to rights and choices (the 'presumption of innocence' notwithstanding). The notion of victims of crime as 'consumers' of justice is more understandable since victims might reasonably regard the cases as 'theirs' and look for a particular outcome to satisfy their interests (perhaps in the form of a compensation award or in the punishment of the offender). Indeed, the rise of victimology is closely linked to the consumerist perspective. At the same time, justice is also dispensed for the benefit of society as a whole, and to this extent society is the 'consumer' (Tuck, 1991).

The application of consumerist principles to criminal justice settings has been seen as a subversive strategy insofar as it involves redefinition of criminal justice as a service industry concerned with customer care rather than a regulatory function of government (Raine and Willson, 1995). More generally, the consumerist reduction of the relationship between public service user and public service provider to one of instrumentalism based on mutual exchange, appears oversimplistic and inappropriate. As James (1994, p. 74) has argued:

> For the relationship between the provider and the user is different in a public service agency. In a free market the customer has a choice whether or not to purchase from a given supplier, given limitations of price, proximity, availability and habit. That choice is essentially a business choice. But the relationship of the service user with the service provider is multi-faceted. It is at one and the same time a financial relationship and a dependent, or at least unequal, relationship.

This has not, however, prevented consumerist thinking being widely and sometimes carelessly applied within criminal justice, with the user being seen as a 'customer'. The court's role, for example, has become judged increasingly in terms of the quality of service and of its responsiveness to the needs and expectations of the other agencies and parties involved in proceedings. In practice, as Raine and Willson (1996) have argued, this has tended to result in a focus on certain aspects of the work of a court (comfort and polite treatment of people) to the relative neglect of others (justice and due process considerations). Arguably, the big issue in relation to consumerism in criminal justice during the period under review has been less about relevance and more about dominance.

5.3 Changes in public voice

A first glance at the development of public voice over the 1980s and 1990s would suggest a shift towards populism – that is, a shift towards more simplistic opinion intended to carry popular appeal. Certainly this was what the Conservative and New Labour politicians were responding to in their speeches and articles in the run-up to the 1997 General Election. As Hough (1996) has argued, a significant change appeared to have taken place from the traditional position: 'Until recently a consensus existed among politicians that the correct response to public opinion was to "manage" it rather than surrender to it' (Hough, 1996, p. 11).

On closer examination, the shift that took place was rather more complex. Public voice, first, tended to get 'noisier' and, second, changed in emphasis. The reasons for both these developments included: first, the perceived failure by the public to have their views adequately represented; second, the emergence of additional opportunities for public presentation and participation; and, third, the channelling of public concerns into certain areas and not others.

Representation of public views

The argument that public voice became 'noisier' during the period under review has been made by Hough (1996). He noted that, between 1970 and 1993, party political differences on criminal justice policy, and hence the need to compete for public consent, were notably absent. Ritual manifesto claims by the Conservatives to be 'the party of law and order', with a few notable initiatives in support of these claims, were realised by exception (for example, the 'short, sharp, shock' experiment of the early 1980s). Indeed criminal justice policy appears to have been conducted largely by a consensus of civil servants, professional practitioners and academic criminologists with 'only the smallest nod in the direction of public opinion' (Hough, 1996, p. 16). Subsequently, a harder line emerged, which Ashworth and Hough (1996) relate partly to the James Bulger case of early 1993. The previous drop in the prison population (from 47,000 to 40,606 between January 1992 and January 1993) was sharply reversed, rising to 45,633 in August 1993 (when the Criminal Justice Act 1993 came into force) and to 47,153 by November 1993.

Hough has ascribed this shift primarily to the judiciary reflecting a change in public opinion. He has argued that this change was bolstered by the media's selective reporting of crimes that would otherwise not have warranted attention; to the media's publicisation of particular views and, crucially, not others; and to reporting practices that tended to disassociate criminal events from their context and hence their relationship to other crime. He has described, in other words, how crime reporting had begun to reconstruct the meaning and significance of crime in the public imagination and had begun to feed fear of crime.

The change of emphasis in public voice during the period was shown by a growing public disillusionment with the capacity or inclination of politicians at local and national levels to represent their views. The increasing disassociation of electoral pledges from actual policy; an apparent unwillingness to consult through the traditional channels of Green and White Papers started under the Thatcher administrations; and, not least, extensive and often trivialised exposure of parliamentary processes to the public through television (for example, Prime Minister's Question Time), coincided with falling polls and general disillusionment with the substance and process of politics in the UK. Coote has described the outcome for the relationship between politicians and public thus:

> Politicians often act as though ordinary members of the public were ignorant or gullible, selfish or irresponsible – or all of these. Of course, if that were so, it would be futile or downright dangerous to involve them in any kind of dialogue. At the same time the voting (and non voting) public tend to assume the whole process of decision-making is hopelessly impermeable, that whatever they do or say will make no difference, and that politicians are driven by self-interest. This mutual distrust serves to

de-skill the people's democratic practice, justifies their exclusion from decision making, and shores up a dysfunctional relationship between politicians and the public. Yet neither view is accurate.

(Coote, 1997, p. 21)

The perceived failure of politicians during the 1980s and 1990s either to represent adequately the agendas regarded as important to the public (for example, ecology or food safety) or to behave in ways deemed appropriate to their status and public profile (prompting the establishment of the Nolan Committee to report on standards in public life) brought into question both the credibility and legitimacy of government itself. This was particularly significant for law and order which, as argued in Chapter 2, undermined the contract between state and citizen; that the one would protect the other in return for allegiance and trust. Loss of public confidence in political representation therefore became a major issue for government.

The response of politicians in the 1990s was to seek to recover public support through identification with overtly populist concerns and attitudes surrounding law and order and criminal justice. By assuming populist views, Ministers presumed that popularity would accompany them. However, in so doing, they were unwittingly undermining the traditional (and mostly unchallenged) assumption that the Government should act in ways felt to be 'in the public interest' rather than as 'representatives of the people'.

New opportunities for public participation

Growing disillusionment with representative modes of democracy and the rise of a more expectant and questioning society combined to create pressure for additional channels and mechanisms for expression of public voice and participation. These included, first, the establishment of new institutions and pressure groups claiming to represent public interest and, second, instances of direct action by members of the public.

Among claims to represent public interest were lobbies and pressure groups. Others included market researchers and the media. The creation of Victim Support and Justice for Victims are examples of alternative representation in the form of pressure groups and lobbies within the criminal justice field. Both organisations were successful in impacting on a mainstream political agenda and were able to create and influence policy in a significant way during the period under review (Chapter 4). The work of Women Against Rape was similarly effective in persuading the police and other institutions to question their assumptions and change their practices in relation to the treatment of rape victims.

More controversial was the claim by sections of the media to represent public opinion. But media-reported crime tended to focus on the most serious and sensational cases rather than presenting a comprehensive picture. Indeed, research has shown that active journalistic imaginations can amplify rather than represent crime, and can produce 'crime waves' (Hall et al., 1978). A more satisfactory explanation of the role of the media is presented by Smith (1987) who suggests that, rather than determining public opinion, the press 'sets the agenda which frames such opinion'. In other words, the media sets the themes around which public opinion is formed. Even this view was challenged with the public response to the death of Diana, Princess of Wales – a response which forced the media to reappraise their opinions of the Princess as represented in headlines in the seven days following the tragedy.

The second outcome of increasing public disillusionment with criminal justice responses was the growing frequency of direct action, of ordinary citizens protesting and resisting policy initiatives and proposals which were 'out of tune' with their own thinking. Representative democracy was increasingly replaced by participative democracy in the last quarter of the twentieth century. This was a transformation that, for example, brought normally law-abiding citizens of all social classes onto the streets to protest vehemently over the Community Charge or Poll Tax, at the export of live animals and new road building. It was the dynamic that also did much to change the Government's approach towards out-of-town supermarket development, and other planning policies. More sombre, but equally telling was the number of people who found themselves on the streets for the funeral of Diana, Princess of Wales, described in the European press as a British revolution through flowers and queues. Direct action was paralleled in criminal justice by roof-top protests at several prisons which put prison conditions more firmly on the public agenda.

Channelling of public concerns

The changing emphasis of public voice reflected the channelling of public concerns into certain areas and crucially not others. The effect was to make public voice heard only selectively in government circles, to reinforce particular public concerns. Perhaps inadvertently, this reinforced a seemingly populist agenda. Examples include the ways in which the agendas – first, around victims and, second, around sentencing – emerged and were handled.

Consideration of victims had historically played a negligible part in judicial process in the UK (Shapland et al., 1985). Paul Rock (1993) identified the marginalisation of victims and their families in court processes; with the victim being treated as the object and the offender as the subject of the offence in an offender-centred procedure. As main witnesses for the prosecution, victims are summonsed to court under threat of a fine or imprisonment for non-compliance, required to give evidence under threat of contempt, can be ruthlessly and demeaningly cross-examined, and not consulted on the sentence or, indeed, on the early release of offenders on parole (Raine and Smith, 1990).

Rock (1990) tracked the ascendancy of the Victim Support movement in Britain from its early foundations in Bristol in the 1970s to that of quasi-state agency, enjoying public funding, working to practice guidelines agreed with the Home Office, the Crown Prosecution Service and other official agencies, and maintaining good relations with politicians, the media and the wider public (see Chapter 4). While the Victim Support movement was important in itself, it is relevant here in the context of public voice. First, it registered dissatisfaction with the ways in which the judicial process was conducted and its outcomes for those involved and, second, it attempted to remedy that dissatisfaction by seeking compensation on an individualistic and case-by-case basis. Underneath what was usually interpreted as a popular and populist concern, lay fundamental discontent with the due process, its outcomes and remedies of law. This presented a considerable challenge both to politicians and to traditional representatives of law and order.

The developing public agenda around sentencing in the 1990s is open to similar interpretation. Researching the populist assumption that the public generally wanted the sentencing of offenders to be tougher, Hough (1996) found little supporting evidence. Taking Court of Appeal judgments as his key indicator of shifts in public opinion (as expressed through the judiciary) he found the public to be 'systematically misinformed' about the levels of sentences imposed and about those actually served in practice. When such misinformation was corrected, he found that public opinion conformed to actual sentencing patterns. His research foun *inconsistency,* rather than *severity,* was the primary issue c cern among those interviewed. The public, when better info ...cu, were more tolerant of the decarceral policies of the 1970s and far from predisposed towards more punitive strategies than conventional wisdom had suggested. Hough (1996) also found that competition between political parties to talk up such strategies was itself a factor in shaping the populist agenda.

5.4 Fear of crime

Common to the issues of the treatment of victims within the criminal justice process and the debate about sentencing, and underpinning both, was public concern over fear of crime. This included fear of being victimised and fear of dangerous criminals in public places. However, having explored the relationship between fear and victimisation, Hale (1996) concluded that fear was only weakly related to the experience of having been a victim oneself. Much more significant in engendering fear of crime was the effect of indirect information about crime, either by word of mouth or through the media which, particularly at local level, often affected people more strongly because they had an affinity with or knew the individual victims whose crimes were vividly described in headlines (Hale, 1996). Important, too, in generating fear of crime was the individual's sense of personal vulnerability, reflecting a range of personal factors, including age, gender and class – factors that would be likely to affect capacity to cope with the psychological, physical and economic effects of crime. This would explain why fear of crime was highest among elderly persons when the risks were highest for young men. Research on fear of crime also highlighted the importance attached to visible symbols of criminality in the immediate vicinity, perceived as indicating broader loss of social control (for example, broken windows and gangs of youths congregating in public places). This was found to be especially significant where residents felt isolated in neighbourhoods which had poorly developed social cohesion and community solidarity. What research on fear of crime also demonstrated was that fear of crime could be counterproductive to neighbourhood safety and that the responses so induced could themselves fuel the risk of victimisation (Hale, 1996).

These findings supported the view that fear of crime was not simply about personal fear of consequence, but about the connection between crime being out of control and a breakdown in social order. Official statistics tended to support this view. Reported instances of violent crime certainly increased year by year, albeit from a relatively low base. More realistic, perhaps, were the findings of the British Crime Surveys, the statistical source based on interviews with samples of the public rather than on police records. These revealed what most people intuitively knew, that the official statistics accounted for a fraction (less than half) of the actual number of crimes committed, the difference being non-reporting (by victims) and non-recording by the police (Home Office, 1996b).

5.5 A revised basis for public voice and participation

An evaluation of changes in public voice, using the six concepts identified at the outset of this chapter, suggests a trend away from participation on the basis of representation and citizenship to participation based on consumerism and potentially on rights. This transition is captured at a broad level in the notion of 'communitarianism', promoted by Amitai Etzioni (1996) and popularised in the UK in Prime Minister Tony Blair's early speeches. However, in communitarianism the complex interaction of responsibilities, civic rights and mutuality within the traditional notion of community are reduced to an image of community primarily held together by income parity and consumer interest. Equity, based on entitlement to political or social benefit, is reduced to the removal of gross inequalities in the ownership of consumer goods and capital.

Within UK public service a similar transition in the nature of participation was to be found in the charter movement of the early 1990s. Like communitarianism, the charter movement was based on a consumerist model and assumed a market ideology. The idea was successful in drawing together a number of different interpretations of public voice and participation. Zedner (1994a) has identified the narrowing of the concept of 'citizenship', which assumes a collective, to 'the citizen', which assumes an individual perspective. She has linked this with the Citizen's Charter initiative (Cabinet

Office, 1992; Chandler, 1996) where the role of the citizen was reconstructed to place it firmly within the marketplace.

> The elaboration of rights to participate equally in the political life of the state and presumption of the means to do so was replaced with specific obligations with little recognition of ideas of political responsibility or social or moral welfare. (Zedner, 1994a, p. 13)

According to Zedner, debates about citizenship became less about rights and more about obligations; less about state responsibilities than personal failure to protect oneself from crime. Examples include the advertising of 'active citizenship' to promote crime prevention campaigns such as Crime Stoppers, and Neighbourhood Watch, which effectively transferred responsibility from the police to local communities.

A similar view has been propounded by Coote (1997), who has commented upon the replacement of substantive rights with procedural rights in the Citizen's Charter. She has argued that the Charter was successful also in accommodating the language of empowerment (as well as citizenship) within the framework of consumerism, in promising service but without participation in service design or delivery. In so doing, she has argued, it promised accountability of form but not of substance.

The shift towards a consumerist perspective in criminal justice was consistent with the general trend in public services towards adopting a market ideology (Bynoe, 1996). This included adopting the term 'police service' over the traditional term 'police force' and the term 'magistrates' courts service' over that of 'magistrates' court'. It was a trend evident in the preoccupation with 'quality of service' initiatives designed mainly to produce improvements in comfort levels for service users.

One group of users who benefited were the victims of crime, who could now expect a more sympathetic reaction from the police, to be kept informed about the progress of their cases, assigned separate waiting facilities at courts, offered emotional support at court, allowed in certain circumstances to give their evidence anonymously through CCTV systems, have their compensation paid more promptly, and be informed of the release of offenders from prison. The new 'customer orientation' extended also to treatment of defendants. At one court, for example, a scheme of 'pre-hearings' was pioneered to provide volunteer assistance to defendants in completing legal aid applications, helping them select a solicitor, make an appointment and explaining the court process (Raine, 1994).

There were clear limits to the pursuit of consumer interests within criminal justice. First, choice – a key component of consumerism – remained decidedly limited. Second, simultaneous with the enhancement of customer services, other traditional rights associated with justice and due process came under threat (for example, the right of defendants to elect trial by jury in 'either way' cases). This suggested a reluctance on the part of practitioners to surrender power to, or authority over, users of service within what remained a coercive context for criminal justice.

In social policy terms the consumerist approach represented a redefinition of equality away from substantive equality (i.e. all persons to be regarded as equal in the eyes of the law) to equality of conditions of service (i.e. all persons to be treated similarly) or, even more simply, to removal of visible signs of inequality of service (i.e. all persons to be seen to be treated similarly).

5.6 Conclusion

This chapter has identified the complex nature of public voice and participation and its emergence as a dynamic in the shaping of criminal justice. Careful examination has demonstrated a complex process of transition taking place behind populist discourse. This was a transition of the expression of public voice based on representation and citizenship to one based on consumerism. In the future there is the potential for further transition towards the expression of public voice based on rights. As a member of the European Union, the UK might be expected to adopt the civil rights and liberties which underpin European legislation. The commitment of the New Labour Government to the adoption of the European Convention on Human Rights would suggest that civil rights will be accompanied by an explicit concern for human rights.

Reflection on the process of transition from public voice based on representation and citizenship to consumerism provides important lessons for criminal justice policy. First, growing disillusionment among the public with the existing means of representation and the subsequent embracing of populist concerns by politicians in order to compete for popularity, tended to underestimate the complexity and significance of public voice, and risked long-term consequences for the credibility of politics and politicians. Listening to the 'noise' of public voice rather than to the concerns which generated it was a doubtful short-term strategy. In a context of an increasingly sophisticated, better-informed and mobilised public, the attachment of politicians to issues of populist concern was a short-term strategy. The ultimate consequences of this strategy would be to undermine the role of the politician as public representative and hence the legitimacy of law and order within a governmental agenda. Responding to public fear of crime, even talking up fear of crime, was also likely to be a short-term strategy since it was bound eventually to be interpreted as failure on the part of government to address crime.

Second, one of the key lessons of the period under review is that policies need to be publicly determined and transparently practised. This is because key decisions in criminal justice tend to be made behind closed doors. For example, decisions to charge are usually made in the privacy of the police custody suite; decisions to prosecute, to offer no evidence or to discontinue, are usually made in the offices of the Crown Prosecution Service; and decisions on verdict and sentence of convicted offenders are usually made in the courts' retiring rooms.

The overwhelming argument for the authentic presentation of public voice in criminal justice is that crime begins and ends in public places. The third and most significant lesson to be drawn from a period of near continuous rising crime and deepening fear of crime is that the problem might not after all be resolved by entrusting the responsibility to government and governmental institutions but depends as much on the contribution of communities and of families. Finding ways of capturing and engaging the complex nature of public voice and participation in appropriate ways within the criminal justice policy-making process and in its practice will prove a prerequisite to the rebuilding of public confidence in addressing crime.

CHAPTER SIX

A revised approach to criminal justice

6.1 Introduction

In Part I of this volume it was argued that the shape of criminal justice in the two decades prior to 1997 owed much to four key dynamics (politics, managerialism, administrative processing and public voice and participation) and to the interaction between them. In Part II (Chapters 6 and 7), the focus shifts to look at the prospects for criminal justice into the millennium. In particular, we consider the nature and size of the space available for policy development, not least by a New Labour administration.

One thing that we can be sure of is that the future will not be a direct continuation of the past, though it is reasonable to expect that the interaction of our four dynamics will provide the basis for whatever transitions and developments take place. In thinking about the future, then, we need to consider, first, how our four dynamics are each likely to alter; second, how their interaction is likely to shift; and, third, how new factors are likely to influence that process. We begin by identifying the conceptual paradigm which underpins Part II. We go on to consider the potential contribution of New Labour, based on reflection on their first year in office. The possibilities and constraints of that contribution are considered through focusing on a case study of youth justice. Youth justice is chosen, first, to ground the discussion in an area of practice and, second, because it represents one of the main challenges for criminal justice policy and one which has become an increasing focus of concern for the Conservatives, for New Labour and for the public. Using youth justice as a 'tracer', the chapter highlights a number of threads which begin to identify the potential for a revised approach to policy development.

6.2 Futures for criminal justice policy

Criminal justice policy, like all social policy, is liable to mood swings. This is because of its political nature, which supports the taking of ideological positions – a process supported by the adversarial culture of party politics. It is also because of the operation of the dynamic of administrative processing (Chapter 4) such that organisational tendencies in large bureaucracies are towards atrophy and homeostasis. This means that change, when it does come, can appear radical and even surprising. In the 1980s and early 1990s these organisational tendencies were reinforced by the introduction of a middle tier of quangos and arms-length agencies which, together with their style of management, served to distance government still further from the practice of criminal justice (Chapter 3). An unintended consequence of this was that necessary and incremental adjustments were less likely to be made as Ministers surrounded themselves with similar-thinking individuals in preference to those professionals, academics and civil servants who had previously provided a significant input to policy-making.

The effect of the mood swing which took place in the early 1990s was such as to amplify the tension between the *justice* and *welfare* paradigms (Chapter 1). Rather than a tension to be managed, the two were set in opposition to one another in the latter years of the Conservative Government, with Michael Howard as Home Secretary.

How to respond to this mood swing, and to the perceived failure of the welfare lobby of the post-war period which it represents, is at the heart of this volume. It also represented the fundamental challenge open to Jack Straw, on becoming Home Secretary on behalf of New Labour. It is appropriate, therefore, to spell out in some detail the range of possible responses and to examine Jack Straw's promises and early interventions into criminal justice immediately prior to the 1997 General Election and on becoming Home Secretary.

One obvious response, as far as the Home Office under New Labour was concerned, was to run actively with the *justice* agenda and specifically with Michael Howard's narrow and retributive version of it. This focused on those individuals apprehended for offending behaviour, through prosecution and sentencing, and particularly through increased use of prison. There are three grounds for objection to this response: first, on values; second, on focus; and third, on financial consequences.

First, on values, the separation of sentencing and penology from its criminal justice context facilitates the implementation of criminal justice penalties without having to take responsibility for the outcomes of those penalties on offenders or on communities. The focus on penalties invites the removal of offenders for the purpose of protecting the public without necessary and appropriate regard for the subsequent reintegration of those offenders after sentence. This in turn facilitates the 'warehousing' rather than reform and personal development of convicted criminals. The conditions of social exclusion which result have the potential to breach basic human rights and social entitlements. This became apparent towards the end of Michael Howard's period at the Home Office. Under financial pressure, and because of overcrowding, commitment to educational, recreational and sporting facilities within prisons was reduced.

Separating penalties from their context can obscure the value base of criminal justice, and this can have wider consequences. Hough (1996) argues that the taste for punishment, once developed, quickly becomes insatiable. The emphasis on incarceration within contemporary criminal justice in California, for example, has become self-reinforcing. David Faulkner (1996) draws similar conclusions, though from a different perspective. He asks what kind of society we wish to live in and therefore what kind of criminal justice is appropriate to support that society? He distinguishes between an 'inclusive' and an 'exclusive' society.

> ... the 'exclusive' view emphasises personal freedom and individual responsibility but is inclined to disregard the influence of situations and circumstances. It distinguishes between a deserving majority who are self-reliant and law-abiding and an under-class – from whom they need to be protected ...
>
> A society which adopts this view is likely to be unsure of itself, suspicious of strangers, hostile towards foreigners and fearful of those who do not conform to its assumptions and stereotypes
>
> (Zedner, 1995)

The contrasting 'inclusive' view is less commonly expressed. It recognises the capacity and will of individuals to change – to improve if they are given guidance, help and encouragement; to be damaged if they are abused or humiliated. It emphasises respect for human dignity and personal identity, and a sense of public duty and social responsibility. It looks more towards putting things right for the future than to allocating blame and awarding punishment, although the latter may sometimes be part of the former ...

The 'inclusive' view is likely to be characteristic of a society which is open and compassionate, which accommodates and respects plurality, and which has some confidence in the future.

(Faulkner, 1996, pp. 5–6)

A second objection centres on the narrowness of focus with its emphasis on penology and fear of crime. The argument about the reducing focus of criminal justice from law and order to sentencing was made in Chapter 2 and will not be reproduced here. In focusing on fear of crime, Michael Howard's agenda drew attention to a problem overly ignored by members of the welfare lobby. But to focus on fear of crime at the expense of evidence of crime was to diagnose the symptom rather than the illness. Arguably the focus reinforced, rather than resolved, levels of fear of crime. It fuelled the argument for the removal of offenders from community settings through custodial sentencing on grounds of public protection. It fed a lust for punishment which could in no way be described as healthy or productive. This resulted in policies based not on resolving crime but on public appeasement for crime, which only escalated the problem. Public appeasement policies were increasingly perceived by the Home Secretary as demanding longer sentences and stiffer penalties for that small proportion of crime (2 per cent) which was successfully processed through the courts (Audit Commission, 1996). For example, the Crime (Sentences) Bill 1997 proposed the abolition of parole and the lengthening of sentences.

Third, critics pointed to the long-term costs of incarceration, the political and economic consequences of which could be compared with the continuing care of the elderly. They claimed that these costs, currently hidden within competitive tendering processes and investment by private companies (through the Private Finance Initiative), would emerge as long-term financial liabilities. This, they argued, would force a policy reversal. For while prison building might be subsidised, once built, prisons, like hotels and elderly persons' homes, would exist to be filled and hence would create self-perpetuating costs. And the muddle over financing long-term care of the elderly suggests that difficult political decisions have, and can be, avoided despite substantial evidence to the contrary. At time of writing, there is little evidence to support a policy reversal. Indeed, the growth of the prison building programme in the UK, as elsewhere, appears strikingly at odds with the resource constraints exercised elsewhere by central government. It is not clear if such financial short-sightedness can be sustained with a New Labour Government committed to the financial constraints of the previous administration for its first two years in office, but wanting to see significant change.

A second response for the Home Office and some practitioners was to sit and wait for these policies to run their course. This can be and has been, the response of various welfare lobbies. One Chief Probation Officer has talked explicitly of

> ... hanging around until the pendulum of retributive/restorative justice swings the other way. (Lockwood, 1997)

> 'Punitive measures don't change behaviour ... they just suppress it', said Gerard Baites, Consultant Forensic Psychiatrist, Norvic Clinic. (Baites, 1997)

> 'In the longer term, prevention must be the best way forward', said Chris Stanley of NACRO. (Baites, 1997)

There is much to be said for sitting and waiting if it means holding the space for alternative presentation of developing views and practices (see the example of Faulkner, 1996). There is much less to be said for it where it freezes intervention or even represents self-interest, as has been suspected of some of the professional lobbies. One thing, however, is certain: there would be no simple return to pre-Howard policies. There would be no going back to a welfare consensus built on Fabian Syndicalism of church, state and judiciary, simply because the context which had created syndicalism and that consensus had long disappeared (see Chapter 2). As the same Chief Probation Officer said,

> This passive stance is rather fatalistic. I really believe that if the pendulum is to swing the other way, it will need leaders in society and heads in organisations to speak out to ensure that happens. (Lockwood, 1997)

This brings us to our third response and the one supported here. Initially perceived as a middle way, this response is arguably more radical than either alternative so far described. It does not begin like the justice lobby from the position of executing justice, and

LIVERPOOL JOHN MOORES UNIVERSITY
LEARNING SERVICES

therefore focused on agencies involved with the apprehension, trial and sentencing of offenders. Nor does it begin like the welfare lobby from the position of offenders, and therefore focused on those professionals whose primary interest is in rehabilitation. It begins rather from the community and from public experience and perception of crime. It begins with the public and the community because it is only here, in the community – not in courts, prisons or government offices – that issues of crime will be resolved (Chapter 5).

The first challenge, then, is to inform and educate a public, which has been 'systematically misinformed' (Hough, 1996), so that public voice can and does represent public opinion on crime and not, as presently, on fear of crime.

The second challenge is to address as a priority the reality of crime as it affects the public and the community – not, as in the justice model, as it affects criminal justice agencies (for example, more police, more stipendiary magistrates), or, as in the welfare model, as it affects the offender (for example, criminalisation) and professionals. This means a focus on public protection, on victims, and on building and sustaining physical and social environments conducive to crime prevention and community support. It means looking again at all those factors which, it is known, make some areas and some people more prone to criminal behaviour than others (for example, poor housing, poverty and unemployment). It means investing in preventative services designed to support and regenerate communities in transition. And it means communities being enabled and funded to provide more support for themselves. It means, in other words, putting criminal justice policy back into social policy.

The third challenge is to address within communities the totality of crime, not simply the small percentage that comes to the attention of the courts nor the even smaller proportion that results in convictions and sentences (Audit Commission, 1996). This means starting from a broad analysis of how and where crime happens, and designing services to meet those realities rather than the other way round. It means an agenda that is needs-led, not service-led.

The fourth, and final, challenge is to redesign and rebalance services to meet those needs, rather than the needs of government departments or of criminal justice agencies. It means, for example, redesigning criminal justice processes to deal more appropriately with the bulk of petty crime, and perhaps, through diversion, allowing the courts more opportunity to focus on serious offences.

This is a challenging agenda for a challenging approach. Although it starts from the public's real experience and perception of crime, it does not necessarily go along with the actions currently demanded to address crime – namely, through penalties in general and incarceration in particular. In effect it seeks to develop actions and responses which are consistent with a context, set of values, policies and ways of practising, and make sense in terms of sustainable policy and practice. In doing so, it seeks not to sit and wait for a change of direction, nor to reinforce and revitalise the justice paradigm, but rather to pick a careful way through what is always a difficult agenda on the understanding that within present experience and practice lie the beginnings of policy for the future. This, then, is the approach behind Part II of this volume and the reasoning behind its form of presentation.

6.3 The interventions of 'New Labour'

It would be easy to exaggerate the potential contribution of a change of government to criminal justice and there is a question about the scope for any administration to change existing practice. Nevertheless, the optimism that pervaded criminal justice immediately after the 1997 General Election appeared to be justified, given a number of seminal announcements from the Home Office in the first few weeks of the new government in office. These suggested a significant freeing up of what, with hindsight, appeared to have become a fixed hand-in-glove or frozen set of relationships.

First came the announcement of one of the most radical constitutional reforms of recent times: the intention to incorporate the European Convention on Human Rights into British law. The new emphasis on human rights was also apparent in the freezing of a string of asylum deportations that had been rushed through at the time of the election and in the declared intention to define a specific new crime of racial harassment. Whether or not these intentions could be delivered, and exactly what in practice would be different as a result, was less certain.

The new Home Secretary quickly took up his predecessor's central debate with the announcement that he would take full responsibility for prisons. This ended the ambiguity between policy-making and operational responsibility for prisons that had been exposed in the events leading up to Michael Howard's sacking of the Director General for Prisons, Derek Lewis, in 1996. Jack Straw engaged quickly with the problem of a rising prison population which, a week before the election, had topped 60,000, the highest number ever. A prison ship had been commissioned from the USA and dropped anchor in Poole harbour ready to house some of those prisoners whom the land-based prisons could no longer accommodate. This was quickly put into service by the new Home Secretary.

While he indicated he was not contemplating the premature release of petty offenders, as a previous Conservative Home Secretary, Douglas Hurd, had done in the 1980s to resolve similar overcrowding problems, it was clear from the outset that Home Secretary, Jack Straw, was looking for ways of reducing the prison population.

Immediately, he announced plans to speed up criminal justice processing by a combination of 'fast tracking' and mandatory time-limits, to reduce the proportion of the prison population on remand and awaiting trial. He asked the Court of Appeal to set sentencing guidelines, to encourage more public debate on sentencing policy and to promote punishment in the community.

> Crown Court judges are using far more custodial sentences than they did, and they lack any collective memory of the crucial decisions they make. Published sentencing guidelines will allow public discussion and understanding of the system. . . . For many non-violent offenders, it would be more sensible to punish them in the community.
>
> (Jack Straw, as reported in *The Independent*, 15 May 1997, p. 12)

It was apparent, too, that behind the scenes the Treasury was pressing Mr Straw in relation to the escalating scale of the prison budget. Less than two weeks into office, and before the Home Secretary had even met formal representatives from the Probation Service, a senior delegation was sent from the Treasury with Home Office officials to view a pilot programme on electronic tagging of offenders at an area probation service.

It is too early to identify a revised approach to criminal justice based on what were a series of very mixed signals and statements of intent emerging in the early months of a new government, rather than evidence of achievement. What can be said is that the 'can do' attitude of 'New Labour' regenerated discourse within the criminal justice sector and stimulated the agencies to begin to re-think their own contributions. Some of the signs of a changing agenda were to be seen in youth justice, which was an issue quick-ly considered by the new Home Secretary, and it provides a power-ful case study of a revised approach under construction.

6.4 A revised approach to youth justice

As Shadow Home Secretary, Jack Straw had supported many of the Conservative Government's measures to deal with crime com-mitted by young people and adopted them when 'New Labour' was elected. To these he added his own list of stringent measures, among which was his call for curfews for children under 10 – a proposal that had earned him the title in the media of the 'child-ren's bogey-man'. After the election, his position seemed hardly to have shifted, and a series of measures were reported to be under active consideration to tackle juvenile crime, including the idea of curfews for under 10s, Saturday schooling for offenders, and or-ders against parents of child offenders. Other measures under con-sideration were: courts to make 'action plan orders' providing detailed schemes to address young offenders' behaviour; the aboli-tion of repeated police cautions and the introduction instead of a new 'final police warning' which would trigger action by multi-agency Youth Offender Teams; out-of-school programmes for youngsters excluded from schools; abolition of the law under which those aged 10–13 are assumed incapable of differentiating right from wrong; and a new child protection order to deal with young children left out unsupervised at night. Many of these pro-posals found their place in the Crime and Disorder Bill, presented to Parliament at the end of 1997.

This, then, was a Home Secretary presenting at least as tough a position as the last.

If he intended to be tough, he also intended to be successful. In choosing ex-Kent Director of Social Services, Norman Warner, as his personal adviser, he chose a hard-headed and innovative indi-vidual who clearly knew the field and who knew that any inter-vention with children and youth would need caring multi-agency support. Warner was invited to lead a Youth Justice Task Force to advise on strategy and help shape the Bill. The work of the Task

Force built on a series of important studies undertaken within the previous year.

Misspent Youth

One of these, entitled 'Misspent Youth', was published by the Audit Commission in November 1996. This was a remarkable study, as much for the way it was conducted as for its brief and findings. Taking two years to produce, and arguably timed with other reports to influence electoral manifestos, it provided a penetrating analysis of expenditure on youth justice which spoke for itself of the need for preventative services. It identified an annual expenditure commitment of £1 billion on processing and dealing with young offenders, of which £660 million was spent by the police. It noted that police began proceedings against two out of every five young offenders apprehended (involving completion of some 40 forms) of whom 50 per cent had their cases withdrawn, discontinued or dismissed (25 per cent) or received a community penalty. Court processes were costing an average of £2,500 for every young person sentenced, and were taking up to 170 days to secure sentence (Audit Commission, 1996). In other words, expenditure was concentrated almost exclusively on those very few individuals who were apprehended, processed through the court and sentenced relative to other cheaper and preventative services. The Audit Commission's obvious recommendation was for a redistribution of expenditure on efficiency grounds. Savings from more efficient processing of detected and prosecuted crime could finance preventative services.

In adopting the 'business case' for redistribution, the Audit Commission neatly side-stepped the ideological minefield of the justice and welfare paradigms, while providing clear evidence in favour of a preventative strategy. The approach paralleled that of developing gender equality where the business case for maximising the human resource potential of women was beginning to be seen to achieve more in practice than approaches based on ideological positions.

Nevertheless, in making its recommendations, the Audit Commission came closer than ever before to extending itself beyond its brief to ensure probity and efficiency of public moneys to making policy recommendations. This was a very delicate line which was carefully managed through a series of consultation meetings with stakeholder groups, both formal and informal, pre-launch seminars and a meticulously constructed launch.

The preventative strategy recommended was important because it provided a stalking horse for entry to a revised approach, represented not by a swing back to the old welfare paradigm with its concentration on social work method, but rather a more balanced approach, arriving at, arguably, welfarist conclusions but from a different and more pragmatic approach. Its recommendations around parenting, schooling, leisure, housing, training and employment and substance abuse, were important because they were grounded in evidence to support the argument for a different distribution of spending priorities.

The way the Audit Commission conducted itself was important. Its skilful use of stakeholder groups ensured that, although Home Secretary Michael Howard immediately distanced himself from the report, it survived and was embraced by those who had participated in its development and in their professional circles. Even more significant was the fact that one of the co-authors of the report was transferred to the Home Office shortly after the General Election and subsequently became Secretary to the Task Force on Youth Justice.

A new three Rs for young offenders

A second report, less influential, but nonetheless significant, was published by NACRO in early 1997. This report gained from being published in the wake of the Audit Commission in promoting a similar approach but this time advocated by a broadly based group from the criminal justice field acting as a multi-agency resource. The report proposed a model that involved young offenders, their families, victims, teachers, and other interested parties working together to identify ways of responding to criminal behaviour that were satisfactory to all parties, held offenders to account and would help in the avoidance of further re-offending.

It looked at the benefits of the Scottish system of 'Children's Hearings' (forums for addressing young people's offending) and also at a 'Family Group Conference' approach in New Zealand and Australia, concluding that each provided models of good practice. A particular strength of these approaches was in restoring damaged relationships between offenders and victims and helping offenders to accept responsibility for their actions and reintegrating themselves into their communities.

As expected from an organisation whose work is focused on working with offenders, the report presented primarily through the eyes of young people involved in crime and had a clear emphasis on prevention, rehabilitation and reintegration. The report was distinctive, however, in articulating a response based on restoration.

> While, as we have seen, in many respects the criminal justice approach expects too much of children and the child welfare approach too little, there is a third way of responding to juvenile offending which offers the prospect of holding juvenile offenders to account much more appropriately, more meaningfully and more actively than the traditional approaches. This is the restorative approach, based on the fundamental premise that an offence is first and foremost an act against another person or the community. Accountability is based on offenders understanding the harm caused by the offences, accepting responsibility for that harm and repairing it. (NACRO, 1997, p. 25)

In so doing, the report made explicit an approach increasingly evident in the actions of criminal justice agencies such as the courts and the Probation Service. The theory of restoration provided a much needed rationale for the increased focus on victims (Chapter 5). It also fitted very well with the consumerist and market-driven ideas of the period, since it was based on the notion of compensation for damage. This was a notion well rehearsed in the American courts in the area of public services.

It fitted rather less well with welfarist notions of preventative solutions presented elsewhere in the report:

> The most important conclusion drawn by the committee is the need for a radical change of direction away from punishment and towards prevention. ... We believe, however, that the underlying theme of preventative policy must be that of tackling social exclusion. (NACRO, 1997, p. 26)

For the restorative theory of justice is, of course, another version of retributive justice or 'lex talionis'. It is based on acknowledgement of guilt and the need for punishment but it permits the substitution of another person or another act in place of punishment. (The theory has been articulated early and explicitly in the biblical story of Abraham's substitution of an animal in place of sacrificing his son, Isaac, and again in the 'scapegoat' placed outside the city walls of ancient Judaea to bear away the confessed misdemeanours of the inhabitants.) It sits therefore rather uncomfortably with notions of preventative welfare and is not necessarily 'more concerned with outcome than intention' as the report claimed.

Having said this, like the Audit Commission study, the NACRO report was distinctly practical in its conclusions and also in its focus on a multi-agency approach. The additional significance in this instance, however, was the strong practitioner representation in the authorship of the report, because it suggested that those in the field, as well as politicians and civil servants, were now looking for alternative approaches and solutions.

Manifesto for Community Safety and Crime Prevention

A third report, with a similar perspective, came from the Local Government Association in the form of a Manifesto for Community Safety and Crime Prevention (Local Government Association, 1997). The focus of this report extended beyond the issue of youth crime, although, given the age profile of offending, many of the arguments in the report were specific to young people.

Like the Audit Commission and NACRO reports, this too adopted a fundamental and wide-ranging approach to the problems of crime and fear of crime. The central argument of the report was for the construction of a policy framework around the notion of 'safer communities'.

> The rebuilding of safer communities extends beyond the creation of local authority-led partnerships. Measures are required to strengthen our idea of citizenship – its rights and responsibilities – and the relationship between citizens and communities.
>
> (Local Government Association, 1997, p. 3)

This was to be achieved through a strategy bringing agencies together at local level to create improvements to the physical and social environment:

> A deterioration of the physical and social fabric of our communities creates a haven within which crime and anti-social

behaviour can flourish. Public spaces that are strewn with rubbish, defaced by graffiti and debilitated by vandalism are profoundly demoralising places in which to live. Social deterioration follows if such spaces are abandoned by the law abiding public, especially after dark. These proposals aim to halt the spiral of decline by marshalling the substantial planning, regulatory and enforcement powers of local government to reclaim a decent physical environment and promote responsible and caring social behaviour.

(Local Government Association, 1997, p. 6)

Not surprisingly, coming from a newly established representative body for local authorities, and at a time close to a General Election, the report advocated a co-ordinating role for local authorities in the preparation of local 'community safety plans'. Like the Audit Commission study, the LGA report emphasised the importance of redirecting funding towards prevention, in this case through the establishment of 'unified local crime budgets' that took account of different agency spending commitments. Again, like its counterparts, the report drew many of its ideas from an analysis of best practice. Its conclusions were reinforced by a set of detailed and practical action points, designed to shape and facilitate implementation. These covered public transport, neglected open spaces, car-parking and traffic management, CCTV, development planning, graffiti and fly-posting, fly-tipping, licensing of premises for entertainment, brothels and prostitution, minicab touting, registration of door attendants and of security firms.

6.5 Case study findings: a revised approach to criminal justice?

With the Task Force on Youth Justice only fairly recently established, it would be premature to pre-empt the conclusions. However, within the three reports presented above, there are some common threads of relevance to the policy development work of the task force.

First, is the holistic approach to problem definition, which was in marked contrast with the distinctly narrow focus of the previous administration. This was in keeping with the approach of systemic management which stressed interaction between functions and organisations. It contrasted with the linear thinking underpinning problem-solving by the single-minded pursuit of objectives: a 'systematic' rather than a 'systems' approach, to problem-solving.

A holistic approach to crime connects it with the social issues of unemployment, housing, poverty and so on. This relocates crime within a broad social policy framework – a location resisted by the Conservative administration on ideological, economic and political grounds. The reconstruction of crime within a social and economic context facilitates a revised approach to addressing the problem. No longer is crime a problem to be solved by criminal justice agencies. Rather it becomes the responsibility of the collectivity of individuals, of parents and teachers, of local communities as well as central government officials and politicians, and is mediated by criminal justice agencies.

This leads to a second thread running across the reports, namely that intervention is seen to demand action at every level and in a variety of ways which are to be locally, as well as nationally, determined. There had already been a number of attempts to reactivate community action and inter-agency action in relation to crime prevention, notably Neighbourhood Watch and the Safer Cities initiatives. Local developments had, however, always been held up by failure at government level to work cross-departmentally, a failure acknowledged and addressed in 'Tackling Drugs Together' in placing co-ordination with a single government department (Home Office, 1994b). The setting up of a cross-departmental sub-committee on the 'Welfare to Work' policy and the assignment of the co-ordinating task for Social Exclusion to a Cabinet Minister Without Portfolio (Peter Mandelson), suggests a more positive approach under New Labour. Whether or not achievement matches intention remains to be seen.

Third, and equally significant for effective intervention, is the forging of a link between tackling crime and the issue of citizenship. All three reports linked community safety with citizenship:

> the rebuilding of safer communities extends beyond the creation of local authority-led partnerships. Measures are required to strengthen our idea of citizenship – its rights and responsibilities – and the relationship between citizens and communities. These proposals provide for new powers and structures designed to curb anti-social behaviour, support the position of young people, tackle serious offending and empower communities to defend themselves against crime.   (Local Government Association, 1997, p. 2)

This view of citizenship goes beyond representative to participatory democracy, beyond involving lay people in the criminal justice process (for example, as jurists or as magistrates) to one about extending public responsibility for criminal offences (for example, making parents responsible for their childrens' offences) and promoting public debate on sentencing and other crime policy issues at community level. In talking about complex problems as 'wicked issues', Clarke and Stewart (1997, p. 6) have argued:

> wicked issues can only begin to be resolved by a style of governing which learns with people and works with people. The wicked issues require a participatory style of governing because the changes have to be owned by people.

A fourth feature common to the reports is the use of an evidence or knowledge-based foundation to the argument. The conclusions of all three reports were rooted in evidence-based practice and adopted a pragmatic focus on 'what works'. This, too, was in contrast with the ideologically charged approach of previous years (though at times evidence was used in the LGA and NACRO reports to support ideology).

The dangers associated with an evidence-based approach are self-evident. First, it promises rationality and prescription in a context characterised more by questions than answers and by dilemmas rather than decisions. Second, it focuses on that which can be proved and that which can be delivered in an environment of aspirations and uncertainties. It has the potential, however, to be something else. Characteristic of the reforms in the wider public sector has been that they were politically driven and implemented by management (Chapters 2 and 3). Nowhere – in health, education, social care and criminal justice – had they been driven by practice. Certainly the reforms had impacted on practice; case management had transformed the way social workers did their jobs; programmes had substantially changed the supervision of practice in the Probation Service; the core curriculum had regulated what teachers were teaching. But in all such examples, the changes were led not by practice but by government or by management. Indeed, the 1980s and early 1990s had been characterised by practice and management growing increasingly apart, with managers being critical of practitioners for not facing up to the realities of resource constraints and, therefore, to the need for greater efficiency and effectiveness. Practitioners had been precious in their response and all too often had adopted a defensive stance in relation to their professional interests.

Evidence-based practice has the potential to turn this tendency on its head. An example of this is the development of a partnership between the Warwickshire Probation Service and Oxford University involving a specially designed case assessment and monitoring system to provide evidence on the effectiveness of different methods of intervention against a set of predetermined performance indicators to inform future practice (Roberts, 1997).

The problem, as the Audit Commission found, was that the effectiveness of criminal justice interventions with young people was rarely measured, and even where it was, the findings were even more rarely used to inform future practice:

> Surprisingly, the effectiveness of different kinds of sentence on re-offending by young people is not assessed on a regular basis in most areas of England and Wales so there is no opportunity to learn from experiences. (Audit Commission, 1996, p. 42)

> Cautioning works well for first offenders and seven out of ten are not known to re-offend within two years (Home Office, 1994). ... But police officers are not trained to issue cautions.
> (Audit Commission, 1996, p. 72)

Changing practice on the basis of evidence of the effectiveness of previous interventions would therefore not be an easy or straightforward task. Work undertaken by the Rowntree Foundation examined four approaches to changing practice behaviour in social care: through training; dissemination of the lessons of evaluated pilots; using consultants; and encouraging champions as innovators. Work by Amanda Sowden (1997) focused on different strategies for bringing about change in individual practice: professional guidelines; educational packs; educational events; reminder systems; personal performance feedback; work with opinion leaders; and better information for service users. Sowden found that the strategy chosen was rarely matched to the identified practice problem.

Within criminal justice there is evidence, not least from the Probation Service, that opening up practice to scrutiny by practitioners themselves, when combined with other initiatives (for example, a drive for research evidence, major changes to professional training and qualification, increased use of targeted programmes to change offending behaviour), is amounting to nothing less than a practice revolution (Underwood, 1997). The key argument in favour of evidence-based practice is that it will eventually force practitioners to use methods that have been found to work rather than those they prefer or in which they were initially trained.

6.6 Summary and conclusion

This chapter has argued for a revised approach to criminal justice – one not based on an ideology of justice or welfare or on policy swings between the two. It has argued for a third way forward, not based on the position of executing justice and therefore focused on those agencies and those professionals concerned with exacting penalty, and not based on the position of the offender and therefore focused on those whose primary interest is welfare and rehabilitation, but based on the position of the community and on public experience and perception of crime. It has argued that, because crime begins here, its resolution must begin here.

Identified within the chapter are four key challenges to progressing this third way: informing and educating public voice; addressing the reality of crime as it affects the public; addressing the totality of crime, and not only that small percentage which reaches the courts; and reinventing services to address the public's needs rather than those of agencies or government departments.

The chapter went on to assess the potential for creating a revised approach for criminal justice and possible support for doing so. It examined critically the space available for the New Labour Government to articulate a revised approach and identified a number of mixed signals emerging from the Home Office in the early days of the new administration. Taking youth justice as a case study, it identified a number of threads common to a series of national reports, significantly with different authorship and addressed to largely different audiences. It concludes that common to a revised approach to criminal justice is an holistic approach to the definition of crime: a multi-layered and multi-faceted approach to intervention; a focus on participatory approaches to citizenship and community in tackling the problem; and a strong basis in evidence of what works. The following chapter goes on to develop that third way, the revised approach.

CHAPTER SEVEN

A future for criminal justice policy

7.1 Introduction

Chapter 6 of this volume argued for a revised approach to criminal justice, based not on either the justice or welfare paradigms but on a 'third way'. That 'third way', it argued, begins from the public experience of crime in the community. The chapter went on to identify possible contemporary threads of such a revised approach using youth justice as a model. Finally it examined the space for action by a 'New Labour' administration and its successors.

Chapter 7 looks beyond contemporary experience and suggests a possible way forward for criminal justice policy. First it identifies a rationale for intervention, a rationale which draws on the heritage of criminal justice in England and Wales, but looks forward to a future within a European context. Second, it suggests a possible strategy for criminal justice based on five key areas of intervention. Again, the strategy builds on and develops contemporary thinking. The chapter, and the volume, close by marking the transition to be made and identifying the key challenges to strategy implementation.

Within this discussion, a possible way forward is presented not as a prescription but rather in the spirit of enquiry, as a contribution among many to contemporary discourse within the complex policy arena of criminal justice.

7.2 A rationale for criminal justice

The existing rationale for criminal justice is based on an ancient and collective contract between the state and its citizens, such that the state promises security (of law and order, of economic protection and of social welfare) in return for allegiance. Chapter 2 detailed the processes by which that contract had been altered and narrowed within criminal justice policy such that its purpose and meaning had arguably become distorted. Chapter 3 described how the careful and difficult balance between executive governmental authority and judicial authority in criminal justice was altered as a result of implementation of managerialist processes of the 1980s and 1990s. Government increasingly assumed an arms-length contractual relationship with criminal justice through delegation of responsibilities. The result was that these agencies increasingly found themselves held accountable for crime, and indeed arguably colluded with the indispensability it implied. In practice, of course, criminal justice agencies were unable to resolve the problem of crime, and were trapped between competing and rising demands placed on them by the Government and the public. While it is legitimate for the state, through government legislation from the Home Office, to delegate a series of tasks to agents of the state and demand accountability for performance and achievement of those tasks, ultimately the responsibility for law and social order remains with the state.

A revised approach to criminal justice requires, first and foremost, the state to take back the responsibility for law and social order, thereby reinstating the contract between the state and the public and making clear the responsibility placed on criminal justice agencies to implement that contract. For it is this fundamental contract of allegiance in return for security which provides the context and the platform for criminal justice policy. In breaching or distorting the contract, the trust between state and people is broken and, hence, intervention takes place in an ideological vacuum – a black hole in which policy initiatives are open to diversion or misunderstanding. Rebuilding the contract will require, at minimum, statements of intent on the part of government, on behalf of the state, and re-negotiation with agencies around what are in reality their delegated and representative accountabilities for intervention.

A revised approach for criminal justice requires, second, the acknowledgement of a second and different kind of contract. This second contract is not top-down between the collective of the people (identified as 'citizens') and the state but lateral between individuals and other individuals. It is a contract not well identified in the UK heritage but commonly found in newer democracies, and typically represented in European legislation on human rights. Under a human rights contract individuals exchange a level of individual right in return for obligations not to abuse the rights of other individuals. While states may adopt or endorse such a contract, rights appertain not primarily due to membership of a state but by virtue of membership of the human race. The state thereby acts not as contractor but as guarantor of a contract between members.

A revised rationale for criminal justice might therefore, it is suggested, be based on two sets of commitments or contracts. The first is a corporate or collective contract between the state and its people, based on the exchange of law and social order for allegiance. The second is a contract between individuals, and endorsed by the state (in the European Convention on Human Rights), whereby individuals exchange rights and responsibilities for and on behalf of each other. Such a rationale would, it is suggested, build on the best of the UK heritage while looking forward to a progressive future within a European context.

7.3 A strategy for criminal justice

Arguing from a framework for criminal justice based on the rationale outlined above, contemporary thinking would point to a strategy for criminal justice founded on five key interventions.

I. Public protection

In his first, brief, presentation on criminal justice policy to the House of Commons (30th July 1997), Labour's Home Secretary used the phrase 'protecting the public' on four occasions. In so doing, his emphasis was consistent with the priority placed on public protection by the public themselves, by the media and by contemporary thinking in criminal justice circles. Protecting the public has to be the first strand in a revised criminal justice strategy because only by being guaranteed safety can the public be enabled to participate in the task of tackling crime. Protecting the public builds, therefore, on the essential contract between the people and the state.

So what do we mean by protecting the public? Under the previous Home Secretary, Michael Howard, the notion of public protection was narrowly identified with the denial of liberty through the increased use of custodial sentences for offenders. This found public support at the time. However, policies of 'zero tolerance' and automatic penalties of imprisonment for repeat offences can, it is argued, escalate danger to the public where suspected offenders perceive themselves as having nothing to lose if convicted (Chapter 1). Indeed, the employment of such policies can be perceived as expressions of fundamental lack of social order and can fuel fear of crime rather than demonstrate public protection. Fear of crime is arguably the contemporary expression not only of fear of direct victimisation, but of that deeper and more profound anxiety about loss of social order (Chapter 5).

To be effective, public protection as a strategy has to be two-sided. It has to address both those who offend and those who are offended against (the latter being citizens in general and victims in particular). In dealing with offenders the aim must be to respond in ways that minimise risks of further offending. In serious cases this may require removal of personal liberty through imprisonment. More often, in the case of persistent offenders, sex offenders and petty offenders, it will involve surveillance and tracking of offenders, sometimes, but not necessarily, in conjunction with other community-based penalties (Zedner, 1994b). This reinforces the role of agencies, not as addressing the impossible task of resolving the problem of crime, but as acting on behalf of the state to enforce the law, with the consent of the public.

But if the public are to consent, they have to know the risks involved. In focusing on the role of the public within a strategy for enhanced public protection, contemporary emphasis is on participants in the criminal justice agencies and in government working with communities in the development of crime prevention approaches, for example, through improved security and surveillance systems for property, Neighbourhood Watch schemes, self-defence classes for women and the like. The evidence is that participation in crime prevention needs to go much further. Effective public protection demands that agencies and government work with the public and their representatives on much more challenging requirements to identify acceptable levels of risk and agree how that is to be managed – for instance, in relation to the resettlement of known paedophile offenders within community settings – in ways that ensure the safety of children. Only by tackling these more difficult issues of risk and dangerousness in informed ways, and being able to trust the transparency and professional responsibility of agencies, will the public feel safe from the threat and fear which accompanies the unknown. Public protection is not simply achieved by removing criminals from public places – which is an expensive and only temporary solution. It is achieved also by ensuring that the public know and accept the levels of risk which they and their families face in going about their daily lives, and are aware that criminal justice agencies are there to manage that risk. This difficult and demanding task, which requires extensive research on risk and offending behaviour, also has implications for the behaviour of the police, the Crown Prosecution Service, the courts, the Probation Service, the prisons and other agencies. It is therefore a task which should not be underestimated and will always be problematic and give rise to error. But the public are much more likely to accept risk if they are informed and involved in the decisions that affect them and can rely on agencies to take their proper part in upholding agreed levels of risk.

2. A broad social policy

Because criminal justice processes intervene only when a crime has been committed or is likely to be committed, they rely on the presence of broad environmental support for their success. Tackling crime through criminal justice processes means, therefore, setting interventions within a broad social policy context capable of achieving acceptable levels of education, employment, housing, health, leisure and environment. We know, for instance, that one of the most effective deterrents to committing crime is having a job (Roberts, 1997), yet job creation and employment initiatives have rarely been pursued within an explicit crime prevention context.

Despite the priority given to prevention in contemporary criminal justice policy, Allen (1997) has argued that the scale of prevention required has been seriously underestimated, with less than 0.5 per cent of the criminal justice budget spent on crime prevention. Home Office statistics reveal that, in 1993–1994, £9.42 billion was spent by government on the criminal justice agencies and only £240 million on direct crime prevention initiatives (Home Office, 1993, 1995). Bright (1997), too, has emphasised this resourcing problem for crime prevention and has argued for 'the institutionalisation of crime prevention through a national strategy' and for substantial new investment. This, he has argued, needs to address the causes of offending behaviour through a broad social policy agenda as well as through traditional methods of making crime more difficult to commit (for example, through increased surveillance, etc.) and of seeking to change attitudes and behaviour of offenders (for example, through rehabilitation programmes and other probation projects for offenders).

Establishing a broad social policy framework within which to view and address the problem of crime forms a crucial component of a revised approach – an approach which is 'problem-based' rather than 'agency-based'. Under this problem-based approach, the challenge is to identify key contemporary problems of crime – drugs, youth crime, alcohol abuse, violent crime, persistent offending – and design strategies and agency responses to resolve them, rather than perpetuate what agencies currently do to contribute to problem resolution (Campbell, 1993, 1997a, 1997b). An example of this approach is the tackling of drugs through an inter-governmental arrangement initiated by New Labour and led by a new drugs 'Czar'. Another is the Welfare-to-Work policy, in which links have explicitly been made with the Home Secretary's strategy for Youth Justice (Straw, 1997).

The problem-based approach to tackling crime fits more appropriately with concerns expressed by the public, who are often puzzled and frustrated by the compartmentalising pattern of responsibilities derived from the separateness of the agencies. It should be distinguished, however, from a 'project-based' approach which is essentially short-term and is designed to promote specific innovations rather than to tackle the long-standing problems which often lie behind particular projects or to replace existing agency functions – though it might in turn act as a catalyst for rethinking these functions in some situations.

3. Community and citizen responsibility

In a context which locates public protection in an integrated social policy, citizens within communities can be enabled to take responsibility for crime and participate in addressing the problem that it represents (Lacey and Zedner, 1995). Outside this context, ten years of research in the UK and the USA has shown that communities lack the capacity to resolve crime and disorder (Bright, 1997). Within this context members of the public can be involved with formal agencies in addressing crime in four different ways: in crime prevention, in community safety, in action on offending behaviour, and in restoration and reconciliation of offenders within the community (Smith, 1987).

Examples of public consultation and participation in relation to *crime prevention* include involvement in initiatives at local level, such as Citizens' Juries and Community Safety Commissions organised by local authorities. In South Lanarkshire, for instance, residents were involved in an initiative piloted by the local council on graffiti and vandalism. Here opinion meters asked local residents about their chief concerns. A Citizens' Jury was then established to address three questions that had emerged from the opinion meter survey. Each was the subject of a day of deliberations by the jury, comprising a representative cross-section of the community (Stewart, 1997). First was the question 'What are the costs of vandalism and graffiti?' (including the social and emotional costs). Second, was the question 'Who is responsible?' (including consideration of the main reasons for the anti-social behaviour). Third was the question 'What can be done?' (with the emphasis on identifying effective preventative approaches). At present Citizens' Juries are being used mainly, as in this example, to provide sponsoring agencies with information and ideas generated in public dialogue. There may be potential to develop the process and implement some of those ideas in conjunction with the public.

In Bath, a different approach was taken. Here the local council established a Safety Commission comprising an independent chair, nine councillors and six co-optees including the local police superintendent, the assistant chief probation officer, the manager of Bath Victim Support, the chair of Bath Racial Equality Council, the manager of Keynsham 'Off the Record' and an academic, all working in close consultation with a range of other interested parties and individuals in the area. Oral evidence was taken from about thirty individuals, about half of whom were officers of the authority and half from relevant organisations; written evidence was received from ten organisations; a conference was held jointly with Crime Concern, attended by a hundred people; contact was established in the field with a Youth Group; a meeting was arranged with representatives of the local magistrates' court; a survey of 600 members of the public was undertaken about their perceptions of crime; the statistics of recorded crime were analysed; and an internal audit was conducted within the council about community safety activities among all departments. Again, the Safety Commission was provided with information and ideas as a result of public consultation. The challenge remains to identify where public consultation can be appropriately converted into public involvement in crime prevention.

There are many examples of citizen involvement in *community safety* in rural as well as urban areas. In Gloucestershire, for instance, following a police decision to reduce the opening hours of the local police station to a limited period each day and to reduce the frequency of patrols, five villages negotiated a scheme to sustain and increase levels of police cover in the area in response to fears about a potential escalation of crime. The parish councils in the area collaborated to establish a rota of volunteers – with police agreement and some basic training and support – to staff the police station, to answer telephone calls and to provide counter services. This had the effect of enabling police officers to spend more time on patrol.

Other examples are of volunteer Parish Wardens and Special Constable schemes operated in conjunction with Neighbourhood Watch or Home Watch schemes (which now cover more than a quarter of the population). Such initiatives are increasingly supported by developments in communications, for example, by the provision of fax and e-mail links between Neighbourhood Watch co-ordinators, parish clerks and the police. In some instances, communities have arranged mobile phone links with local beat officers to hasten response times when incidents arise.

There are fewer examples, as yet, of community involvement in *action with offenders*, not least because of reservations by professionals working in criminal justice agencies. Successful schemes include the Southampton Appropriate Adult Scheme, where volunteers are trained to accompany those detained for offences during police interviews where mental illness is suspected. Another example is the scheme mentioned in Chapter 5, jointly organised by Bexley magistrates' court and the local Volunteer Bureau. Here, volunteers attend court to provide assistance to defendants in completing legal aid application forms, in choosing a solicitor to represent them, in making appointments and generally advising on the court process.

More widespread is the opportunity for citizen involvement in criminal justice as lay magistrates, jurists or probation volunteers. There are more than 30,000 lay magistrates, providing an opportunity for some people to contribute to criminal justice and public protection at local level. The main obstacle to expanding such participation is the current terms of service under which magistrates are appointed. Usually people are appointed in their thirties or forties and are expected to sit for at least one day each fortnight until the statutory retirement age of 70. This excludes many people on the grounds that they are unable to give the time while maintaining careers and domestic responsibilities. More flexible recruitment rules and terms of service – for example, by allowing shorter periods of service on the local bench or different patterns of sittings (say, a full-time block of one month per year, rather than one day per fortnight) – would make joining the magistracy more accessible. This would, in turn, help to build ties with the community and confidence in the work of the local bench. Similarly, it could be beneficial to increase volunteer contributions on a part-time basis to community service work with offenders under the auspices of the Probation Service or their voluntary sector partners.

There is room, too, for more public involvement in the *restoration and reconciliation* of offenders within the community (Burnside, 1994). Presently much of this work involves victims and the part-time volunteers who meet with them. Indeed, there is some concern that the focus on victims and victimology is unwittingly confining the concept and scope of restoration to reparation between individual victims (or their representatives) and offenders, to the neglect of reconciliation with the community. The concept of reconciliation was made explicit by the early church missionary ancestors of the Probation Service who had the task of taking offenders out of the hands of the courts and restoring them to the community. A more recent professional example comes from NACRO (Chapter 6) with its recommendation for Family Conferencing as practised in New Zealand (NACRO, 1997). Drawing on the Scottish experience of Children's Panels for young offenders, NACRO has recommended a follow-through to agree reparation between offenders and victims, victims' families or the community, depending on the nature of the offence. This approach has attracted much interest in the UK and has been taken up by Thames Valley Police in a pioneering scheme in Aylesbury, Buckinghamshire (*The Independent*, 18 October 1997). Here, during 1996, around 170 offenders who would previously have been cautioned were required to attend 'community conferences' with their victims and to acknowledge the harm caused, often apologising and offering to make amends. Victims were given a choice whether or not to take part, but most chose to do so. The sessions, which typically lasted for between half an hour and two hours, were often very difficult for the offenders, particularly with the necessary presence of parents or relatives. They were effective to the extent that they provided opportunity for offenders to confront the consequences of crime and to repair damage. The sessions also proved very helpful to some victims in explaining what had happened and why, hence reducing fear. It is an approach that is likely to be adopted more widely.

Taken together, the contribution of the public in crime prevention, in community safety, action on offending behaviour and in restoration and reconciliation in the community can be perceived as an imaginative strategy for social inclusion; a concept much to the fore in European Union social policy and seemingly adopted by the New Labour Government in 1997.

4. Tackling offenders

Central to a revised strategy for criminal justice is the need to tackle offending in ways which reinforce the individual's responsibility for individual behaviour. This requires three sets of activities. First, it requires the targeting of specific responses to clearly identified educational and employment needs. Research conducted by Warwickshire Probation Service and the University of Oxford Probation Studies Unit indicated that, of offenders studied, having a job was the single most important factor in avoiding re-offending. It is also a key factor in successful resettlement and social inclusion (Roberts, 1997).

Less obvious, but equally significant, is the downward spiral effected by poor education and lack of job prospects. Colin Pritchard (1997) has identified the significance of school exclusion in promoting careers in crime by triggering a series of other exclusions from peer groups, from the community and from the workplace. Similar analyses by Birmingham City Education Department (Bignall, 1997) have revealed common themes of deteriorating achievement among black children in school, from being among the highest achieving groups in the early years of primary school to the lowest at GCSE level, and their subsequent over-representation in the crime statistics. In turn the Department has identified a range of actions designed to minimise the occurrence of school exclusions, through better monitoring, the establishment of a specialist School Exclusions Team of officers and a Working Party of elected members. At the same time attention is being directed at correcting under-achievement through mentoring schemes, summer schools and improved school attendance monitoring. These examples reinforce the Labour Government's 'Welfare to Work', Youth Justice, New Deal and education programmes.

Second, responses to individual offending behaviour need to be clearly targeted and evaluated to achieve agreed outcomes. Such targeting relies on an effective assessment of risk, on the availability of a variety of interventions (including supervision, surveillance, training programmes and custodial sentencing) and on clear evaluation of success and failure. The 'what works' research of the Probation Service is relevant here, including that of Andrew Underwood at the Home Office (Underwood, 1997).

Third, tackling offending behaviour requires a firm and fair approach to prosecution and to sanctions for persistent and serious crime. A priority here is to address the tendency for charges in some serious cases to be down-graded by police and prosecutors in order to save time and money in the court process while achieving a safe conviction. Another would be to develop further guidance to sentencers (for example, from the Magistrates' Association) to ensure greater consistency in the approach to setting penalties in serious cases. Custody is necessary and appropriate in some circumstances and offenders need to know that.

5. Organisational reform

Reform of the agencies and institutions which, together, represent criminal justice is the fifth and final strand in a strategy for criminal justice. It is fifth because agency reform is a consequence of the other four strands. This is in contrast with organisational reform in criminal justice over the past two decades when, in the absence of a broad strategic approach, the focus has been on organisational and fiscal reform. Together with the substantial volume of new legislation, the consequence of such reform has been largely structural in effect and managerial in character (Chapter 3).

The introduction of limited pluralisation of providers (state, private and voluntary sector providers), together with a broader range of provision (custody, surveillance, community penalties), has introduced a new level of complexity into criminal justice arrangements. Previously there was a clear and direct link between the state and its providers, mediated by the public administration (for example, between the Home Office and the prisons) and between the judiciary and the offender (for example, at the court). One effect of changing the nature and range of provision has been to require a broader set of activities at the public administration level to co-ordinate demand and supply among different providers, to monitor quality and efficiency, and to address complaints and allegations of abuse against providers. Thus the role of the public administration has been enhanced to provide the operational framework required to facilitate complex service provision. In turn, the operational framework has been reinforced by support services, mainly of three kinds: educational (revision of validation and training requirements), professional (enhancement of professional associations) and inspectorial (development of inspectorates). The Probation Service, for example, has experienced redrafting of professional and managerial training requirements; enhanced acknowledgement of the Association of Chief Officers of Probation (ACOP) in dialogue with Ministers; and separate identification and development of a central Inspectorate for Probation.

Owing to this complexity, the experience of agencies working within the enhanced operational framework now provided under the Home Office, or within government agencies, has been of overload with an increasing required level of response (for example, to legislation, circulars, inspection reports, etc.) perceived as centralisation.

If the nature of organisational arrangements has been characterised by complexity, it has also been subject to rapid change as individual agencies have sought, or have been required, to adjust their functions and activities to meet a changing set of identified social conditions and social problems. Drugs, for example, which lie behind much individual and organised crime, remain the responsibility of every agency and of no agency. The difficulty remains about how to engage a variety of agencies in tackling serious and new problem conditions, including youth justice and social exclusion. This has usually been resolved by the identification of a leading agency, and much energy has gone into competing for leadership (for example, of youth justice via the Youth Justice Task Force, 1997).

This 'problem-centred' approach to crime resolution has important consequences for the organisation of existing agencies in criminal justice. As more and more problems are identified as cutting across existing agency boundaries, the existing and distinctive functions of individual agencies begin to take on a residual character.

Thus, these two features of complexity and cross-cutting problems raise important questions for the future organisation of criminal justice agencies. The present challenge is not how to turn agencies into a criminal justice system, but rather how to manage the transition from agency-based to problem-based functions while still maintaining the distinct purposes of different agencies – purposes which are rightly characterised as much by independence and an adversarial model as by a systemic model. This points to an holistic review of criminal justice organisation in response to pluralisation of services and the identification of new social problems. It points less to a set of individual responses by individual agencies. Indeed, it points away from a strategy based on restructuring agencies (based on geographical area or merged functions) towards one based on building capacity for responsiveness.

7.4 Managing transition

Identification of a rationale and of five key areas of strategic intervention raises important issues about the nature of the transition to be made in criminal justice as a whole. First, the revised approach builds on both the 'justice' and 'welfare' paradigms. It is firm in relation to offending behaviour; penalties must be strictly enforced and the authority of the law consistently upheld. There can be no soft options allowed here. It is because of such firmness that the approach would be able to attend to the human rights of offenders. Conversely, its firmness would rely on a social welfare paradigm being applied not simply to individual offenders, but to the social fabric of society as a whole. Its intention must be to build an inclusive society.

Second, it would mark a significant rebalancing of energies between responding to crime once it has occurred and investing in crime prevention in the broadest sense.

Third, it would imply a problem-centred, rather than an agency-centred or offender-centred, approach to tackling crime. Agencies would be redesigned or required to work together strategically and proactively on agreed problems in consultation and in conjunction with the public at local level.

Finally, it would put responsibility for addressing the crime problem back where it belongs, not only with criminal justice agencies, but with offenders, parents, teachers, employers and local communities and their leaders.

7.5 Conclusion

This book has posed three questions: What is the contemporary purpose of criminal justice? What influences have shaped criminal justice in recent years? What does this discussion tell us about criminal justice for the future?

In discussing the influences which have shaped criminal justice in recent years, Part I of this volume (Chapters 2–5) has argued the presence and interplay of four dynamics (politicisation, managerialism, administrative processing and public voice and participation). In thinking about criminal justice for the future, Part II has rehearsed the key features of a revised approach (Chapter 6) and a set of priorities: informing and educating public voice and participation; addressing the reality of crime as it affects the public; addressing the totality of crime, not just that small proportion which reaches the courts; and redesigning and rebalancing the organisation of criminal justice to address the requirements of an informed public rather than those of the official agencies and government departments. Finally, Chapter 7 has gone on to present a possible way forward in the interests of dialogue and discussion.

The extent to which a revised approach emerges for criminal justice depends on developments with regard to each of the four dynamics. Each has the potential to (a) contribute towards the realisation of a more effective criminal justice process and (b) address the crime problem.

The dynamic of *politicisation* is clearly important; fresh direction from political leaders is necessary to move on from the narrow preoccupation with sentencing and punishment of recent years towards a new vision for tackling crime and for relocating criminal justice firmly in its social policy context. It is also vital in the renegotiation of the 'contract' between the state and its people about a shared responsibility for crime.

The dynamic of *managerialism* – though problematic because of the tendency for management to become regarded as an end in itself rather than part of the means by which criminal justice is done better – is also important for the future. Significant weaknesses about the pre-managerial way of doing things have been highlighted and challenged. Much of the complacency and inertia of the past, particularly regarding the way the agencies have approached their responsibilities, has been driven out. The momentum for change that managerialism has created will remain an important attribute underpinning a revised approach to criminal justice. In particular, a revised approach depends on sustaining and developing those legacies of managerialism: needs-driven rather than provider-driven services, more transparency and stronger public accountability, and a focus on effectiveness and outcomes (on 'what works').

The *administrative processing* dynamic, though also in some ways associated with negative attributes of inertia and resistance to change, of organisational fragmentation, and of undue provider-orientation, is important to the revised approach. It provides the key to the translation of policy into practice. Its focus on the practitioners and on how criminal justice works in practice means that it is potentially a very important dynamic in relation to local communities being empowered to take responsibility for crime and encouraged to participate more actively in tackling the problem. The challenge is for practitioners to reorient their work and their organisational and administrative processes so that a stronger relationship with, and accountability to, local communities is achieved.

This brings us to the *public voice and participation* dynamic, which is perhaps the most important key to realisation of the revised approach. Above all, the revised approach builds upon the notion that tackling crime should begin with the reality of crime as it is experienced by the public and as it affects them. The challenge here is to find ways of capturing and engaging the full complexity of public voice and participation in appropriate ways within the criminal justice policy-making process and in its practice.

What, then, is the contemporary purpose of criminal justice? The conclusion from this volume is that first, it remains that identified in the ancient contract between the people and the state – namely, the provision of security in exchange for allegiance. Second, and relevant to the position of the UK in Europe, it is the protection of individual human rights (as presently represented in the European Convention on Human Rights, and endorsed by the Labour Government in 1997).

Recapturing that ancient purpose, and making explicit that new purpose, is the fundamental prerequisite to the rebuilding of trust in the criminal justice agencies and in government on law and order. It is also a prerequisite to public confidence in the view that crime is not, after all, out of control and that there are constructive approaches to be pursued, based on a partnership between the state and its people, which will make a difference.

References

Allen R (1997) *Children and Crime: Taking Responsibility*, London: Institute for Public Policy Research

Ashworth A (1994) *The Criminal Process: An Evaluative Study*, Oxford: Clarendon Press

Ashworth A and Hough M (1996) Sentencing and the Climate of Opinion, *Criminal Law Review*, pp. 776–87

Audit Commission (1996) *Misspent Youth: Young People and Crime*, London: Audit Commission

Baites G (1997) quoted in Stanley C, Exceptions to the Rule, *Community Care*, 29 May, p. 10

Barron A and Scott C (1992) The Citizen's Charter Programme, *Modern Law Review*, 55, 526

Bell D (1974) *The Coming of Post-Industrial Society*, New York: Basic Books

Bignall B (1997) *School Exclusion and Youth Crime*, Paper presented at a Conference on Youth Justice, Institute of Local Government Studies: University of Birmingham

Boswell G (1995) *Violent Victims*, London: The Prince's Trust

Bright J (1997) *Turning the Tide*, London: DEMOS

Burnside J (1994) *Relational Justice: Repairing the Breach*, Winchester: Waterside Press

Bynoe I (1996) *Beyond the Citizen's Charter*, London: Institute for Public Policy Research

Cabinet Office (1989) *Improving Management in Government: The Next Steps*, London: HMSO

Cabinet Office (1992) *The Citizen's Charter*, London: HMSO

Campbell B (1993) *Goliath*, London: Methuen

Campbell B (1997a) Consider the Children, *Community Care*, 9 January, p. 12

Campbell B (1997b) Metaphorically Speaking, *Community Care*, 12 June, p. 20

Chandler J A (1996) *The Citizen's Charter*, London: Dartmouth

Clarke J, Cochrane A and McLaughlin E (1994) *Managing Social Policy*, London: Sage

Clarke M and Stewart J (1997) *Handling the Wicked Issues*, School of Public Policy Occasional Paper, University of Birmingham

Coote A (1997) An Optical Illusion, *Community Care*, 6 March, p. 21

Davies M, Croall H and Tyrer J (1995) *Criminal Justice: An Introduction to the Criminal Justice System in England and Wales*, Harlow: Longman

Department for Education and Employment (1995) *National Survey of Local Education Authorities' Policies and Procedures for the Identification of the Provision for Children who are Out of School by Reason of Exclusion or Otherwise*, London: DfEE

Downes D (1997) What the Government Should Do About Crime, *The Howard Journal*, 36 (1), 1–13

Drucker P (1954) *The Practice of Management*, New York: Harper Bros

Dunleavy P (1994) Globalisation of Public Services, *Public Policy and Administration*, Autumn, pp. 123–42

Easton M and Rawlings A (1995) The Citizen's Charter and the Criminal Justice System, in Willett D (ed.) *The Citizen's Charter*, London: Macmillan

Etzioni A (1996) *The Spirit of Community: Rights, Responsibilities and the Communitarian Age*, London: Fontana

Faulkner D (1994) *Law and Citizenship: Rights, Duties and Control*, A Series of Seminars, St John's College, Oxford

Faulkner D (1996) *Darkness and Light: Justice, Crime and Management for Today*, London: Howard League

Field S and Thomas P A (1994) *Justice and Efficiency?*, The Royal Commission on Criminal Justice, Oxford: Blackwell

Foster C and Plowden F (1996) *The State Under Stress*, Milton Keynes: Open University Press

Foucault M (1986) *Foucault Reader* in Rabinow P (ed.), London: Penguin

Foucault M (1997) *Discipline and Punishment*, London: Macmillan

Freidson E (1970) *Profession of Medicine: A Study of the Sociology of Applied Knowledge*, New York: Dodd, Mead & Co

Garland D (1996) The Limits of the Sovereign State: Strategies of Crime Control in Contemporary Society, *British Journal of Criminology*, Autumn, pp. 445–71

Graham J and Bowling G (1995) Young People and Crime, Home Office Research Study No. 45, London, Home Office

Hale C (1996) Fear of Crime: A Review of the Literature, *International Review of Victimology*, vol. 4, pp. 79–150

Hall S, Critcher C, Jefferson T, Clarke J and Roberts B (1978) *Policing the Crisis: Mugging, the State and Law and Order*, London: Macmillan

Harden I (1992) *The Contracting State*, Milton Keynes: Open University Press

HM Magistrates' Courts Service Inspectorate (1996) *Annual Report of Her Majesty's Chief Inspector of the Magistrates' Courts Service*, London: HMSO

Home Office (1981) *Report of the Royal Commission on Criminal Procedure*, London: Home Office

Home Office (1984) *The Police and Criminal Evidence Act, 1984*, London: Home Office

Home Office (1985) *Magistrates' Courts (Advance Information) Rules*, London: Home Office

Home Office (1989) *Magistrates' Courts: Report of a Scrutiny*, London: Home Office

Home Office (1990) *Punishment, Custody and the Community*, Cm 424, London: HMSO

Home Office (1993) *A Practical Guide to Crime Prevention for Local Partnerships*, London: Home Office

Home Office (1994a) *The Police and Magistrates' Courts Act, 1994*

Home Office (1994b) *Tackling Drugs Together: A Consultation Document on a Strategy for England 1995–1998*, Cm 2678, London: HMSO

Home Office (1995) *Information on the Criminal Justice System*, London: Home Office Research and Statistics Division

Home Office (1996a) *The Victim's Charter. A Statement of Service Standards for Victims of Crime*, London: Home Office

Home Office (1996b) *The 1996 British Crime Survey: England and Wales*, London: Home Office

Home Office (1997) *Review of Delay in the Criminal Justice System* (Narey Report), London: Home Office

Home Office and Department of Health (1996) *Probation and Health: A Guidance Document Aimed at Promoting Effective Working Between the Health and Probation Services*, London: HMSO

Hood C (1991) A Public Management For All Seasons?, *Public Administration*, 69 (1), 3–19

Hough M (1996) People Talking about Punishment, *The Howard Journal*, 35 (3), 191–214

Hutton W (1995) *The State We're In*, London: Jonathan Cape

Independent, The (1997) Jack Straw as reported, on 15 May, p. 12

James A (1994) *Managing to Care: Public Service and the Market*, London: Longman

James A (1996) *Life on the Edge. Diversion and the Mentally Disordered Offender*, London: Mental Health Foundation

James A (1997) Beyond the Market in Public Service, *Journal of Medicine and Management*, 11 (1), 43–50

Jones C (1993) Auditing Criminal Justice, *British Journal of Criminology*, 33 (3), 45–52

Lacey N (1994) Government as Manager, Citizen as Consumer: The Case of the Criminal Justice Act 1991, *Modern Law Review*, 57(4), pp. 534–54

Lacey N and Zedner L (1995) Discourses of Community in Criminal Justice, *Journal of Law and Society*, 22 (3)

Langan P (1991) Between Prisons and Probation: Intermediate Sanctions, *Science*, vol 264, p. 791

Le Grand J (1990) *Quasi-Markets and Social Policy: Studies in Decentralisation and Quasi-Markets*, Bristol: School for Advanced Urban Studies, University of Bristol

Leishman F, Loveday B and Savage S P (eds) (1996) *Core Issues in Policing*, London: Longman

Levitt S (1996) The Effect of Prison Population Size on Crime Rates, *Quarterly Journal of Economics*, vol. 3, pp. 319–52

Local Government Association (1997) *Manifesto for Community Safety and Crime Prevention*, London: LGA

Lockwood H (1997) *The Myth of Justice*, Paper presented to the Chief Officers of Probation Learning Set, September, London

Lord Chancellor's Department (1992) *A New Framework for Local Justice*, London: Lord Chancellor's Department

Mayhew P, Mirrlees-Black C and Aye Maung N (1994) *Trends in Crime: Findings from the 1992 British Crime Survey*, Research Findings No. 14, London: Home Research and Statistics Directorate

McConville M, Sanders A and Leng R (1991) *The Case for the Prosecution*, London: Routledge

McLaughlin E and Muncie J (eds) (1996) *Controlling Crime*, London: Sage

Magistrates' Association (1997) *Sentencing Guidelines*, London: Magistrates' Association

Marris A (1996) *The Politics of Uncertainty: Attachment in Public and Private Life*, London: Routledge

Mirrlees-Black C (1994) *Estimating the Extent of Domestic Violence: Findings from the 1992 British Crime Survey*, Research Findings No. 9, London: Home Office Research and Statistics Directorate

MORI (1996) *Public Opinion in Britain*, London: MORI

Muncie J and McLaughlin E (eds) (1996) *The Problem of Crime*, London: Sage

Murray C (1990) *The Emerging British Underclass*, London: Institute for Economic Affairs

Murray C (1994), *The Underclass: The Crisis Deepens*, London: Institute for Economic Affairs

Murray C (1997) *Does Prison Work?* London: The IEA Health and Welfare Unit

NACRO (1997) *A New Three Rs for Young Offenders: Towards a New Strategy for Children Who Offend*, London: National Association for the Care and Resettlement of Offenders

New York Times (1997) Leader Article, 5 July

Newburn T (1995) *Crime and Criminal Justice Policy*, Harlow: Longman

Newman J and Clarke J (1994) Going about our Business? The Managerialisation of Public Services, in Clarke J, Cochrane A and McLaughlin E (eds) *Managing Social Policy*, London: Sage

Nolan (1997) *Report of the Committee on Standards in Public Life*, London: HMSO

Osborne, D and Gaebler T (1992) *Reinventing Government*, Massachusetts: Addison Wesley

Penal Affairs Consortium (1997) *The Crime (Sentences) Bill*, London: Penal Affairs Consortium

Pfeffer N and Coote A (1991) *Is Quality Good For You?* Social Policy Paper No. 5, London: Institute for Public Policy Research

Pollitt C (1990) *Managerialism and the Public Services: The Anglo-American Experience*, Oxford: Blackwell

Potter J (1988) Consumerism and the Public Services: How Well Does the Coat Fit?, *Public Administration*, 66, 2, 149–64

Pritchard C (1997) *Reducing Truancy and Delinquency: A Family–Teacher–Social Work Alliance*, The Programme Development Unit, Home Office, London: HMSO

Raine J W (1994) *Ready to Proceed: An Evaluation of Early Administrative Hearings at Bexley Magistrates' Court*, London: Home Office

Raine J W and Smith R (1990) *The Victim and Witness in Court*, London: National Association of Victim Support Schemes

Raine J W and Willson M J (1993) *Managing Criminal Justice*, Hemel Hempstead: Harvester Wheatsheaf

Raine J W and Willson M J (1995) New Public Management and Criminal Justice, *Public Money and Management*, 15 (1), 35–40

Raine J W and Willson M J (1996) Beyond Managerialism in Criminal Justice, *Howard Journal*, 36 (1), 80–95

Raine J W and Willson M J (1997) Police Bail With Conditions: The Use, Misuse and Consequences of a New Police Power, *British Journal of Criminology*, No. 4, pp. 296–312

Reiner R (1992) *The Politics of the Police*, Brighton: Harvester

Reynolds M (1991) *Crime in Texas*, Dallas: National Center for Policy Analysis

Roberts C (1997) *Evaluating Supervision Practice: Report on a Pilot Project*; Oxford: Institute of Criminology

Rock P (1990) *Helping Victims of Crime: The Home Office and the Rise of Victim Support in England and Wales*, Oxford: Clarendon Press

REFERENCES

Rock P (1993) *The Social World of an English Crown Court*, Oxford: Clarendon Press

Rowntree B S (1902) *Poverty – A Study of Town Life* (2nd Edition), London: Macmillan

Runciman (1993) *Report of the Royal Commission on Criminal Justice*, Cm 2263, London: HMSO

Rutherford A (1993) *Criminal Justice and the Pursuit of Decency*, Oxford: Oxford University Press

Rutherford A (1997) Beyond Crime Control, in Murray C (1997) *Does Prison Work?*, London IEA Health and Welfare Unit

Ryan M and Ward T (1989) *Privatisation and the Penal System: the American Experience and the Debate in Britain*, Milton Keynes: Open University Press

Shapland J, Willmore J and Duff P (1985) *Victims in the Criminal Justice System*, Aldershot: Gower

Smith D (1987) Research, the Community and the Police, in Willmott P (ed.) *Policing and the Community*, London: Policy Studies Institute

Sowden A (1997) *How Individuals Learn and Change, in Bringing About Change in Practice*, Report of a Seminar hosted by the Joseph Rowntree Foundation, York

Stanley C (1997) Exceptions to the Rule, *Community Care*, 29 May, p. 10

Stewart J (1997) *Innovation in Democratic Practice*, Occasional Paper, School of Public Policy, University of Birmingham

Stewart J and Walsh K (1992) Change in the Management of Public Services, *Public Administration*, 70 (4), 499–518

Straw J (1997) *Improving the Effectiveness of the Criminal Justice System*, Press Release on the Statement by the Home Secretary to the House of Commons, 30 July 1997, London: Home Office

Tuck M (1991) Community and the Criminal Justice System, *Policy Studies*, 12, pp. 22–29

Uglow S (1995) *Criminal Justice*, London: Sweet & Maxwell

Underwood A (1997) *Effective Supervision*, Her Majesty's Inspectorate of Probation, London: Home Office

Walsh K (1995) *Public Services and Market Mechanisms*, London: Macmillan

Wasik M and Taylor R (1994) *The Criminal Justice Act, 1991*, London: Blackstone Press

Wilson J Q (1975) *Thinking About Crime*, New York: Basic Books

Woolf (1991) *Prison Disturbances, April 1990: Report of an Inquiry*, Cm 1456, London: HMSO

Young J (1997) Charles Murray and the American Prison Experiment: The Dilemmas of a Libertarian, in Murray C (1997) *Does Prison Work?*, London IEA Health and Welfare Unit

Zedner L (1993) *The Dynamics of Justice*, London: The Howard League

Zedner L (1994a) *The Limits of Law Enforcement*, Seminar Paper to the Law and Citizenship Conference, St John's College, Oxford

Zedner L (1994b) *Should Sentencers Use Imprisonment So Readily as a Response to Offending Behaviour?*, Paper presented at the Howard League Conference, London: Wormwood Scrubs

Zedner L (1995) In Pursuit of the Vernacular: Comparing Law and Order Discourse in Britian and Germany, *Social and Legal Studies*, vol 4, pp. 16–31

Index